L. Delaney's All Dolled Up

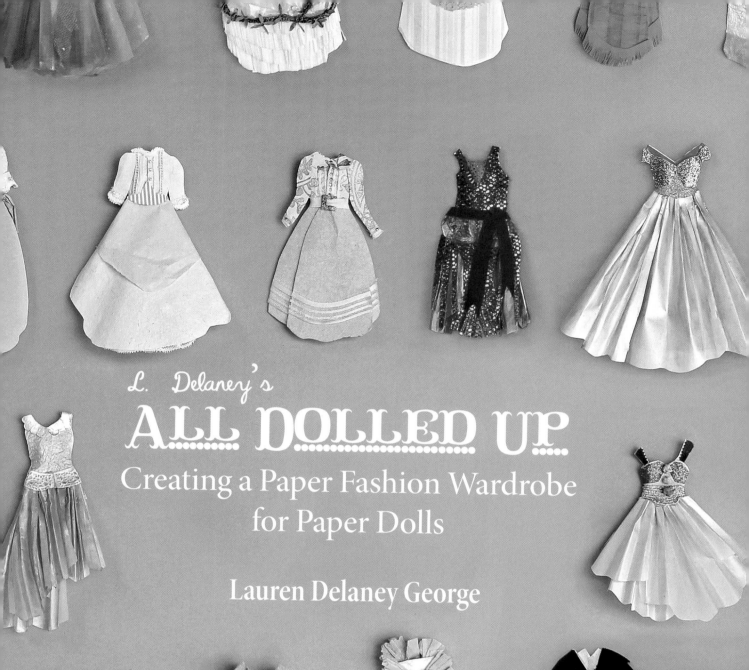

L. Delaney's
ALL DOLLED UP
Creating a Paper Fashion Wardrobe
for Paper Dolls

Lauren Delaney George

Dover Publications, Inc., Mineola, New York

To Grandpa Geno and his Kate

Bibliographical Note
L. Delaney's All Dolled Up: Creating a Paper Fashion Wardrobe for Paper Dolls
is a new work, first published by Dover Publications, Inc., in 2017.

International Standard Book Number
ISBN-13: 978-0-486-81080-5
ISBN-10: 0-486-81080-1

Manufactured in the United States by LSC Communications
81080101 2017
www.doverpublications.com

CONTENTS

In the attic
where the rain touched the
roof softly on Spring days
and where you could feel the
mantle of snow outside, a few
inches away, on December nights,

A Thousand Times Great Grandmere existed.
—Ray Bradbury

Introduction: The Magic in Old Clothes

Nothing is more evocative—or intimate—than clothing. It projects both personality and circumstance, shielding and deceiving both the wearer and the watcher. It is filled with ghosts.

These ghosts answer to "History" and "Imagination." The garments they inhabit are gossamer bridges to a past alive with romance, laughter, and heartbreak. The ghosts tug at hems, whispering secrets to those who would listen.

Long before I could interpret decades in a hemline, I read a story about two girls snooping around a witch's closet. By some Narnia-like magic, the closet extended backward, containing centuries of clothing. In high school I was enthralled to rediscover this magic in the costume storage of Kalamazoo's Civic Theatre, an inexhaustible cache of clothing whose every stitch was a character to be brought to life on stage. As a costume designer, I harness clothing's transformative power as a form of storytelling. You only need to observe a busy sidewalk for an hour to know that this is true. With varying degrees of self-awareness, we all wear costumes, revealing and obfuscating evolving identities.

Contemporary devotees of antique clothing borrow from previous generations for a self-expression unbounded by the decades. The current nostalgia for fashion is fed by TV shows such as *Downton Abbey* and vintage glamazons like Dita Von Teese. Now, more than ever, we play dress-up in our mothers', grandmothers', and great-grandmothers' attics. When we unlock the attic's mysterious armoire in this book, we learn about ourselves.

L. Delaney's All Dolled Up is a love letter to the women whose dresses now gather dust in antique shops and attics. It tells the story of Lucille and Reo, but it's really your story to tell: of the women in your life who blazed trails, raised families, lived and loved. Inspiration and adventure don't live only in attics: They greet you around every corner, in portraits hanging on museum walls, in old films, and in your own family's photo albums. Live the kind of story you'd like to tell: Bring it to life and movement through your craft.

The armoire in this story was sculpted from a tattered lace collar. I wonder about the Victorian woman whose hands created it. Though she would be unfamiliar with a hot glue gun, I'd like to think that she would enjoy flipping through these pages. I hope that the coats you create for her will have secrets hidden in the pockets for her granddaughters to discover.

Lauren George
New Orleans
May 2016

The Old Armoire

When I was little, my family made trips to Detroit to visit my Great-Aunt Lucille. While the adults chatted, my sister and I would explore Lucille's house, burrowing into the library and tracing our names into dust-covered artifacts. As we sank into our beds, Lucille told us stories about Grandma Reo. Reo and Lucille traveled widely, breathing the air of unfamiliar places. The soft edges of our sleep were rounded by Lucille's silvery whisper as she recalled the fantastic scenes of their adventures. That the sisters had once been brave explorers—happily covered in mud or "all dolled up"—seemed a far cry from the old woman sitting beside us now. When we grew older, we assumed that her incredible stories were more fairy tale than truth.

But then we discovered the armoire.

When Lucille passed away, we were called back to her home to tie up the ends of a long life. Tucked among the trinkets and family photographs was a key. We were familiar with the attic's ancient—and locked—armoire. Now we brushed aside cobwebs to turn the key in its rusted lock. As the heavy doors creaked open, moths the size of birds tumbled out. We began to pull out its secrets. . . .

Dresses, hats, and fur coats. Blouses and trousers. Threadbare shoes that had traveled many miles. The rustling taffeta and satin whispered stories of Lucille and Reo. Here was the dress Reo had performed in aboard the famous Mississippi showboat . . . and there were the boots that had carried Lucille across the Rocky Mountains. Silks, leathers, and laces: An orchestra of frills and texture bringing Lucille's stories to life in vivid technicolor.

Now I'll tell you the story, just as Great-Aunt Lucille told it to us. But I should warn you: this is not a story of well-behaved women.

Family Parlor

Our story begins with a pair of cold feet.

On her wedding day, Reo happened to catch a glimpse of a passing circus. While family and guests sat waiting in the church, those foolish girls hit the road.

How-To: Pages 37-41

Canvas City

As the circus train carried Reo and Lucille across the Midwest, they learned the arts of knife throwing, snake-charming, and beard-growing from their strange new companions. Reo and Lucille soon developed their own acts. Reo wowed the crowds with her knife-throwing. Lucille and the Circus Beast—a much-maligned species of Kalamazoo garter snake—made a charming duo. When the circus performed in St. Louis, the girls were spotted by the captain of a showboat. Captain Ravenal invited them to join his troupe of actors floating down the Mississippi.

PREBLE & SONS
PRESENT WILD WEIRD
WONDERFUL HUMANS

Nothing like ever it seen

How-To: Pages 42-46

Cotton Blossom

Once a riverboat gambler, Captain Ravenal had put all of his poker winnings into the *Cotton Blossom*. Daily, the floating theater would dock in a new port, and the actors and band would disembark, parading through town to announce the evening's shows. As dusk fell across the river, people would make their way down to the levee amid the glowing lights stringing the *Cotton Blossom*'s deck.

The girls spent a jolly season, meeting ne'er-do-wells and adventure seekers. From the decks of their drifting home, they glimpsed ever-changing worlds of blue and green. One day, the *Cotton Blossom* came to a curious bend in the Mississippi.

How-To: Pages 47-52

New Orleans

After bidding farewell to their companions aboard the *Cotton Blossom,* Reo and Lucille set off into the heart of New Orleans' French Quarter. The sisters had never been to a more enchanting—or enchanted—city!

Soon they made the acquaintance of Miss Lizzy Breaux, descended from Russian Tsars. The girls taught Lizzy to throw knives and play Faro—a game taught to them by the riverboat gamblers. Lizzy, thoroughly amused by her new friends, invited them to join her for the season's whirl of Mardi Gras balls.

Sweeping onto St. Charles Avenue one night, Reo and Lucille stumbled right into the path of the city's most famous voodoo queen, who issued a strange proclamation: The sisters had many miles to travel before they reached their home. They packed their things and regretfully departed.

How-To: Pages 53-56

Western Skies

Leaving New Orleans, the sisters made their way west. As swamp turned to desert, they happened upon a group of travelers headed in the opposite direction: Wildcat Kirkham's Famous Western Show!

Chivalrous and brave, Wildcat Kirkham was the richest man alive—if wealth were measured in Rocky Mountain sunsets and the friendship of a mule named Amos. Wildcat traveled from town to town with his buckaroo pals, re-enacting scenes out of a wilder West. Their most popular act was a thrilling tribute to the legendary frontiersman Davy Crockett.

Wildcat's posse included sharpshooter Ada Rose. With the face of an angel and the mouth of a sailor, Ada could split a playing card held edge-on at ninety paces. When she promised to teach the girls how to shoot, they decided to head east with their new friends. Of all their marvelous adventures, the girls' enjoyment of life was never keener than on those nights spent beneath the Milky Way, listening to the coyotes howl—even better than any tea or ballroom party.

How-To: Pages 57-61

Dreamland

Wildcat's gang was scheduled to perform at New York City's sparkling new amusement park, Dreamland. Illuminated by no fewer than one million electric bulbs, Dreamland was a cardboard fantasy conjured for park-goers, who could float in gondolas through an imitation Venice, witness the eruption of Mount Vesuvius, and take a trip to the moon. To its exotic performing animals—and even more exotic human beings—Dreamland was also home.

While Wildcat and his gang performed "The Great Train Robbery" in the park's arena, Lucille and Reo became mermaid and diver in a submarine ride to Atlantis. They lived there happily until a fire erupted one evening in an adjacent ride. Flames licked at the pasteboard landscape and, within an hour, the marvelous playground had been reduced to smoldering ash. Lucille and Reo would return to the strange cardboard city in their dreams: its colors and sights at once magical, fantastic, and absurd.

In the fire's aftermath, Lucille and Reo encountered the famous reporter Nina Bell. Striking up a rapport—and out of work—they made plans to join her on her next adventure. Just like that, the sisters found themselves traipsing across the Antarctic.

How-To: Pages 62-67

Explorers' Club

By the time that Lucille and Reo made Nina Bell's acquaintance, she'd caused quite a stir in the world of journalism. Nina had been catapulted to national fame after feigning insanity and infiltrating a lunatic asylum. After the release of her best-selling exposé, she turned her sights to setting records by pushing the boundaries of exploration.

Since New York's famed Explorers' Club was closed to women, the trio set off across the globe: The "Race for the South Pole" was afoot between the explorers Amundsen and Scott, and the girls decided to show the world that women were equally fit for adventure. After trudging miles across an unforgiving landscape, Reo lost several toes to frostbite, and although the Amundsen expedition beat the girls to the South Pole, their bravery was applauded. They now turned their sights to aviation, and landed squarely in the middle of the "barnstorming" craze.

How-To: Pages 68-71

High Flight

Reo and Lucille discovered a new form of entertainment sweeping the country: stunt aviation. Not wanting to be left behind, they wasted no time enrolling in flying lessons. With each ascent to the clouds, their flying became more skilled. Reo mastered "wing walking," and Lucille discovered a fondness for the "loop-de-loop."

The girls began to perform in a "flying circus"—a brave fleet of aviators traveling from town to town, turning cornfields into runways and competing with each other in ever-increasing acts of daring. Sweeping the sun-cleft clouds, the sisters defied death as they wowed the crowds below.

Reo and Lucille then made the acquaintance of an eccentric character who shared their love of aviation. When autumn ended their performance season, they returned with him to Detroit, where he was scheduled to attend the séance of a famed psychic. Their new friend and aviation enthusiast was none other than the magician Harry Houdini! Houdini had dabbled in aviation, setting several world records as casually as one might make morning tea. Now he set his sights on a different challenge—debunking the many hucksters posing as psychics in the latest craze of "spiritualism."

How-To: Pages 72-76

Séance Parlor

And so the girls found themselves back in Detroit, seated at the séance table of the famed occultist Montague Rhodes. Houdini had revealed his method of attending séances while in costume, accompanied by a reporter and a police officer. At a critical moment in the "super-natural" proceedings, Houdini would leap up and unmask the imposter's ghostly trickery.

After so many adventures, the girls were delighted to be back in their home city, where Reo made a blushing apology to her jilted beau. But soon their feet were restless for the road. Where would their feet take them next?

How-To: Pages 77-81

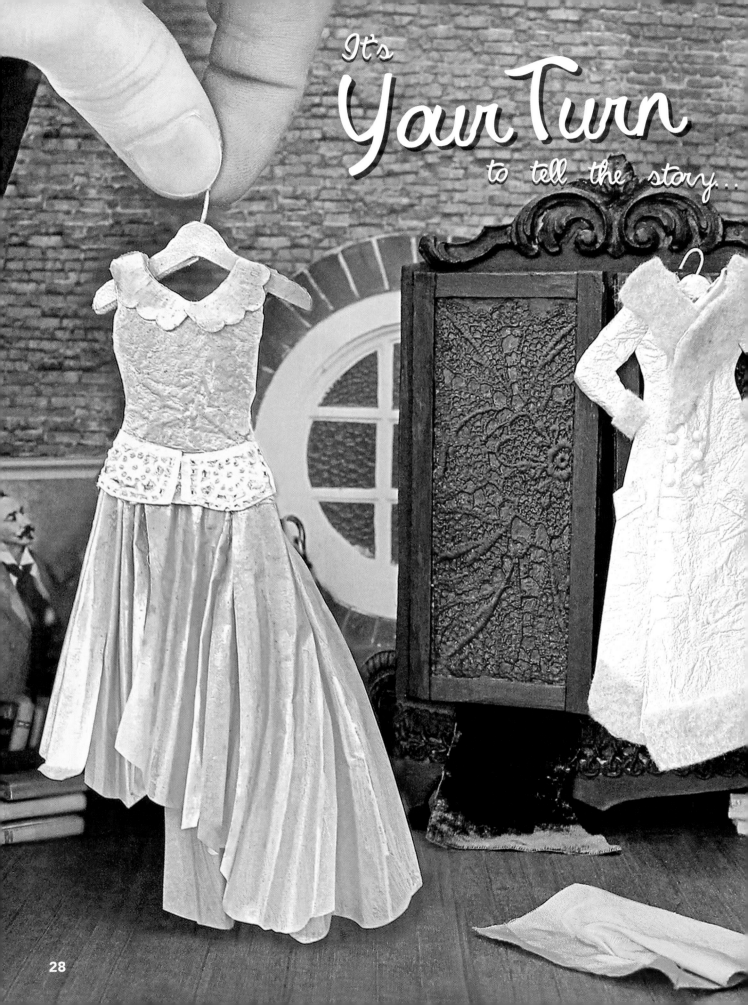

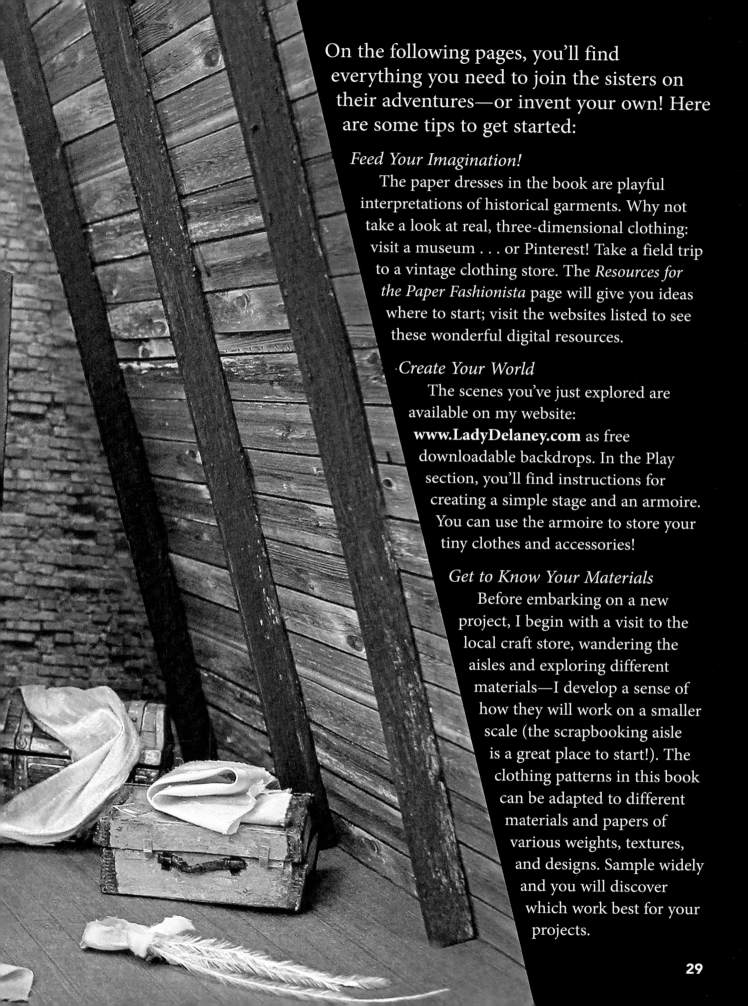

On the following pages, you'll find everything you need to join the sisters on their adventures—or invent your own! Here are some tips to get started:

Feed Your Imagination!

The paper dresses in the book are playful interpretations of historical garments. Why not take a look at real, three-dimensional clothing: visit a museum . . . or Pinterest! Take a field trip to a vintage clothing store. The *Resources for the Paper Fashionista* page will give you ideas where to start; visit the websites listed to see these wonderful digital resources.

Create Your World

The scenes you've just explored are available on my website: **www.LadyDelaney.com** as free downloadable backdrops. In the Play section, you'll find instructions for creating a simple stage and an armoire. You can use the armoire to store your tiny clothes and accessories!

Get to Know Your Materials

Before embarking on a new project, I begin with a visit to the local craft store, wandering the aisles and exploring different materials—I develop a sense of how they will work on a smaller scale (the scrapbooking aisle is a great place to start!). The clothing patterns in this book can be adapted to different materials and papers of various weights, textures, and designs. Sample widely and you will discover which work best for your projects.

Materials

To begin splendifying your paper dolls, look no farther than the scrap pile! When possible, the exact paint colors, paper products, and embellishments used for each outfit have been listed at the start of its respective How-To. *But don't be afraid to improvise.* My working philosophy is that the best material is whatever I have on hand. Almost everything can be substituted; in a pinch, I'll even use nail polish as paint!

Tools

The tools required won't vary much between projects; you can bet your bloomers that a hot glue gun, craft glue, scissors, acrylic paint, and a paintbrush will always come in handy.

Paper

Tissue paper, wrapping paper, cardstock paper, and . . . toilet paper? There is almost no limit to the materials you can adapt for use in your miniature art. The paper fashionista blazes fearlessly ahead, experimenting with every paper in her path!

Paint

When it comes to art supplies, more expensive *does not always mean better,* and this is definitely true for paint. My strategy is to keep a limited assortment of acrylics, which I then mix for custom colors. I use everything from Martha Stewart's hues to $1 bottles of Americana®. I love the FolkArt® and DecoArt® lines of metallics, and I generally find any iridescent pastel paint to be irresistible! If you have difficulty mixing paints, brush up on your knowledge of the color wheel.

I use paintbrushes recklessly, so I like to keep stocked with the cheap variety packs.

Vintage Remnants

These dresses are the perfect repurposing for tattered vintage lace, ribbon, and other materials otherwise destined for the garbage. Antique stores are filled with such treasures, and you could get lost digging through bits and pieces of old sewing notions for the perfect embellishment. The wonderful thing about working on such a small scale is that you need very little material. Supplies for your tiny art don't have to break the bank!

Adhesives

These projects call for several different kinds of adhesives. When you require something strong and fast-drying for structural draping, reach (carefully) for the hot glue! And though its sticking power isn't as strong as hot glue, an Elmer's® glue stick works nicely for covering large areas with little fuss. Liquid craft glue like Delta Sobo® or Aleene's® is stronger than an Elmer's glue stick and takes longer to dry than hot glue, making it ideal for attaching smaller (and nonporous) decorative elements. Use a fine paintbrush to apply it, and be glad that it dries clear, hiding all manner of mess!

To attach the finished dresses to the dolls, you may want to consider a *nonpermanent adhesive*. Depending on your purpose, rubber cement, glue tape, glue dots, clothespins, or paper clips may all be options.

Et Cetera

Any of the following materials may also be useful to the paper dressmaker:

- antique ephemera
- family photos
- fashion research
- photocopier
- tracing paper
- No. 2 pencils
- colored pencils
- feathers
- scrapbook embellishments
- adhesive gemstones
- craft glue
- acrylic paint
- paint palette
- storage for custom paint colors
- hot glue
- hot glue sticks
- tape (double + single sided)
- glitter and metallic paint
- needles
- thread
- paper scissors
- embroidery scissors
- hole puncher
- decorative paper punches
- decorative edge scissors

- assorted paintbrushes
- silk flower petals
- floral remnants
- paper scraps
- vellum paper
- tissue paper
- scrapbooking + decorative paper
- old wallpaper
- decorative cocktail napkins
- medium-gauge metal wire
- small X-ACTO® blade
- gold doilies
- multi-color doilies
- nail polish
- nail decals
- confetti
- felt
- lace
- ribbon
- rick rack
- glitter
- paper towel
- clothespins/paper clips

Before You Begin...

Each How-To section begins with a short introduction and includes a materials list, photographic key, and ideas for further research. The photographic key will show you which paper was used for each pattern piece. Before you begin, read through the steps; this will help you to pick appropriate materials and avoid "hiccups."

Create Workable Templates

To achieve dimensionality in your paper clothing, the How-Tos require you to sculpt it directly onto a *copy* of the doll. *So before you begin crafting the outfits, you'll need to duplicate the paper dolls.* You can photocopy them onto white cardstock (or similarly heavy) paper. This can be done on a home copier and doesn't have to be high resolution, or even in color! Once you have finished, trim the doll copy away from the completed garment. Attach the garment to your original doll using a nonpermanent adhesive. But don't fret if you don't have access to a photocopier; you can transfer the doll silhouette to cardstock using good old tracing paper!

To create your doll form using cardstock and tracing paper:
1. Place a piece of tracing paper over the doll and use a pencil to outline her body, excluding the hands, head, and feet. 2. Cut the shape you have created from the tracing paper. 3. Place the tracing paper silhouette right side down onto a piece of cardstock and trace around it. 4. Cut out the cardstock doll form. This form will be the base for your paper garment-making. Choose the How-To you'd like to try, and create your outfit by sculpting and gluing it directly to this form.

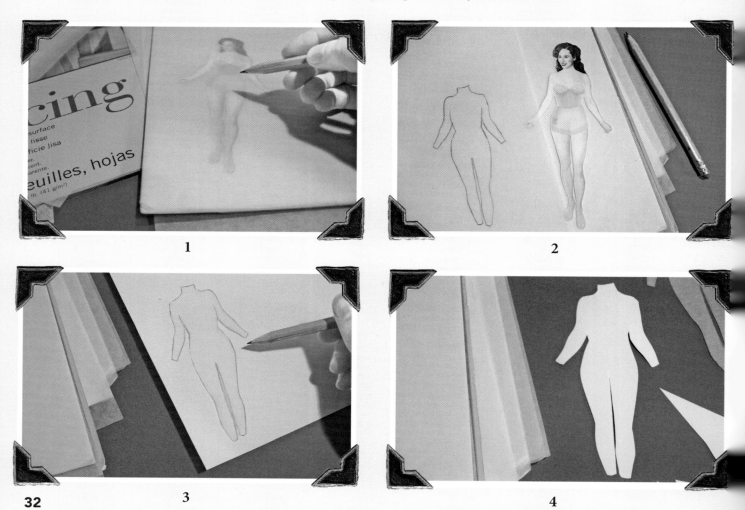

1

2

3

4

Create Workable Templates (Cont.).

If you photocopy the paper dolls rather than trace them, these finishing steps will get them ready for the How-Tos. After you have cut out Lucille, **carefully** use a sharp X-ACTO® blade to remove the white space between her arms and midsection (don't let children try this without supervision!). A self-healing cutting mat will protect your work surface from damage. The X-ACTO® will also be useful for the corners of the doll that are tricky to snip with scissors.

Many of the How-Tos require you to drape material around the dolls' necks, so make a small snip in your photocopy where the hair meets the shoulders. In the case of your Lucille photocopy, use your scissors to separate her hands from her hips. This will make it easier to drape around her waist. Note that it is *not* necessary to make these snips to the original dolls, just to the photocopies.

Prepare Your Pattern Pieces.

As with the dolls, copying the pattern pieces will maximize the book's usability. Photocopying them will always be faster and more accurate, but if that's not an option, tracing paper and pencil will do the trick! Transferring the pattern pieces to a heavy paper like cardstock will give them longer life.

You'll notice that the pattern pieces are color coordinated to their respective dolls. If you are photocopying them, you can do so in low-resolution black/white mode, which tends to be less expensive. Once you have cut out the pattern pieces, keep them organized in small envelopes or plastic bags.

To copy the pattern pieces by tracing:
1. Place a piece of tracing paper over the pattern page and outline its shapes in pencil. 2. Cut out your tracing paper copies, labeling the side with the pencil outline as the front and making a note of which pattern piece this is.

3. To cut out the garment pieces, place the paper with the fancy side facedown, and the pattern piece on top, with its text facedown.

1   2   3

Always *place the pattern piece with its front (text side) against the back of your chosen paper. Trace it in pencil.*

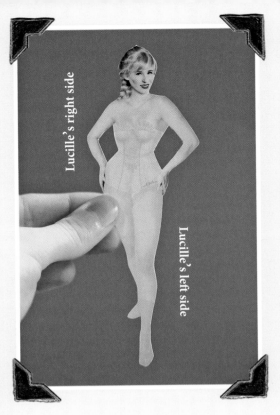

Lucille's right side

Lucille's left side

Get Yourself Oriented.

The How-Tos often will refer to a doll's left or right side. Keep in mind that this is *in relation to the doll's body, rather than the crafter's*. To prevent confusion, this will be consistent throughout the tutorials. Each How-To step is also accompanied by a photo, making it easier to get back on track if you get confused.

Reduce or Enlarge Your Dolls (optional).

The benefit of using a photocopier is that you can change the size of your paper dolls. Since photocopiers—even most home photocopiers—offer reduction and enlargement settings, you can play with scaling your copies to more or less than 100% of their original size. Be sure to use the sturdy cardstock when creating your small (or big) copies. Note that as you reduce or enlarge your dolls, the image's quality will change. The larger the percentage of reduction/enlargement, the more drastic the change in quality.

The pattern pieces in this book are scaled for use with the paper dolls as given. Should you choose to modify the dolls' size, remember to scale the pattern pieces accordingly. If you decide to play with sculpting clothing in different scales, you may discover that a material that works well in one scale may not work in another. It will take some trial and error to find what works best. For example, a smaller dress may be more realistically achieved with a very thin material like tissue paper. There is no limit to the worlds you can explore!

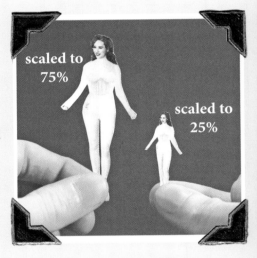

scaled to 75%

scaled to 25%

Read This if You Get Discouraged.

Inevitably, coffee gets spilled on a project or glue gets gunky; pieces are cut the wrong way and feelings of frustration creep in. When this happens to me, I take a deep breath and step away for an hour. Watching something silly on TV or getting some inspiration via Pinterest allows me to return to the problem with renewed ideas and enthusiasm. And you will! More often than not, the solution to your problem simply requires a set of fresh eyes. Even something as simple as washing the glue and paint from your hands can reset your focus.

Inspiration will jump out at you from around strange corners indeed! In the case of the spilled coffee (or paint), maybe that little splash of color was just what your project needed—let your eyes be open to the possibilities. One of the most valuable lessons I learned was taught to me by a set designer. Struggling to move forward with a stage design, he threw some materials into his tiny theatrical model in frustration. Seeing their haphazard arrangement suddenly jogged the creative part of his brain, and he was back on track! This example demonstrates that sometimes moving forward requires a bit of a mess.

The activities in this book are ideally suited to that scrap pile growing in your craft corner. And for the sculptor of scraps, risk is minimal! You can mess up as many times as you need to get it right. As you tackle the How-Tos, remember that there is always a learning curve with new techniques. Hiccups in your process mean that you are learning the limitations of your materials.

Paper Draping 101

The art of draping is a classic component of fashion design. For this book, the concept has been adapted to paper. In the preceding pages you learned to prepare the form on which to sculpt your paper garment—much as a clothing designer uses a dress form. As you'll soon see, your paper draping will achieve the *illusion* of a full dress, while only creating the front half!

As you work your way through the How-Tos, imagine your creations as sculptural representations of real clothing. Observing the drape of historical garments will help you capture its dimensionality in another medium. Whether draping fabric or paper, *it's all about finding a balance between controlling the material and letting it do what it wants*—it's a playful conversation between designer and material.

Lili Vintage Boutique, New Orleans 2016

Lili Vintage Boutique, New Orleans 2016

Lucille's bridesmaid dress, Detroit 1888

Choose the Drape, Not the Paper

Just like real fabrics, every paper is going to sculpt differently from the next. Your material's observable properties will help you to anticipate its drape. Note its shine, how stiff or flexible it is, and its thickness. Understanding these qualities will help you to work with it, rather than against it.

When draping, don't stress too much about each individual fold! Embrace the "accidents" and think big picture. Just remember that you are draping—not wrestling!!

As you drape your paper pieces, consider their relationship to the other materials. Ribbon, lace, and flower petals will add beautiful interest to a piece and highlight fine drapework!

Drape for Dimensionality.

The outfits in this book depart from a traditional model of flat paper doll fashion. Turning paper into dimensional garments requires a bit more time and planning. You'll notice that the pattern pieces for the clothing are slightly larger than the dolls themselves. This will allow you to shape the piece so that it sits slightly away from the doll's body, assisting the illusion of a lady underneath!

When the paper you are using is thick, shape it a bit before gluing it into place. This is especially true for bodice and skirt pieces. For the striped bodice piece below, a glue stick comes in handy for this technique.

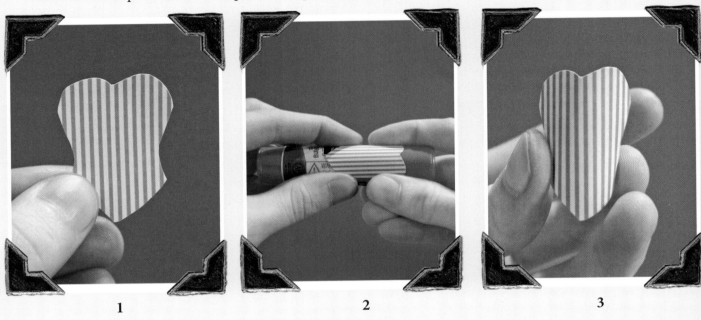

1   2   3

Create a Stand for Your Doll Form

As you are draping, you may find it helpful to occasionally set the doll in a standing position, step back, and survey your progress. An easy stand for your form can be created using 10" of medium-gauge wire. Bend half of the wire into a loop and tape the straight part of the wire to the back of your doll. A 2-ounce paint bottle set on the metal loop will stabilize it nicely!

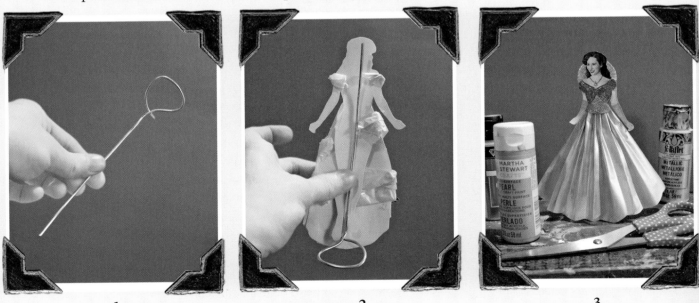

1   2   3

If you don't care as much about dimensionality or want to use the garments for scrapbooking, glue the garment pieces flat to the dolls and trim the excess. This would be an appropriate modification for younger or less experienced papercrafters!

Family Parlor

EQUIPMENT

hot glue gun
hot glue sticks
craft glue
scissors
paintbrush
acrylic paint
paper doll duplicates
Family Parlor templates

Step into the family parlor, where the sisters are preparing for Reo's wedding!

The girls had planned to trot down the chapel aisle in style; their dresses are the very height of early 1880s fashion. Research the gowns designed by Charles Frederick Worth, one of the late nineteenth century's most famous couturièrs—the elegance of Worth's dresses comes from a play between structure and drape. Note the bell-shaped skirt, sufficiently aerodynamic for chapel escapes!

When cutting your pieces from the provided templates, remember to always trace them so that the side of the template with text is against the *back* of your chosen paper!

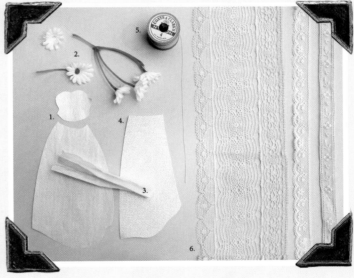

MATERIALS: REO

1. The Paper Studio® Silk Pearlescent paper
2. The Paper Studio® Swirl Pearlescent paper
3. The Paper Studio® Stripe Pearlescent paper
4. The Paper Studio® Crepe-White paper
5. iridescent white tissue paper
6. white thread
7. The Paper Studio® Spare Parts White Micro Roses
8. green floral remnants
9. The Paper Studio® Gemstones Small Pearl

MATERIALS: LUCILLE

1. iridescent cream paper
2. tiny silk daisies
3. pale blue tissue paper
4. iridescent white paper with crosshatch texture
5. pale blue thread
6. antique lace

FolkArt® Pearl White Metallic Acrylic Paint [not shown]

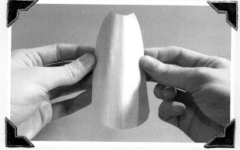

1. Gently flex Reo's skirt piece to give it a bit of dimension. When you are finished, the piece should curve a bit, rather than lying flat. Hold the skirt against Reo and fold the top corners of the skirt so that they hug her hips.

2. Once you are happy with your skirt's position and dimensionality, anchor it to the doll form by running your hot glue gun along the *edge* and back of her hips. Be careful not to flatten the skirt as you secure it to the hot glue.

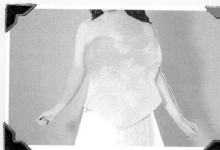

3. Run a thin line of hot glue along the doll's right abdomen. Place the bodice in the glue so that its edge lines up with the edge of the doll. The other side of the bodice should now be hanging over the doll's left abdomen, as if it was too large.

4. Push the unglued edge of the bodice towards the center of the doll's abdomen and secure it with hot glue. This should cause the bodice piece to buckle out in the middle.

5. Point your hot glue gun into the bodice cleavage, applying a generous amount of hot glue. Before the glue has hardened, push the protruding bodice into the glue, creating two ridges.

6. Now Reo may not be Dolly Parton, but at least she's got a little something! This is a good time to cut any excess bodice paper at the doll's sides to keep her waist trim.

7. Apply craft glue to the triangular bodice insert with your paintbrush and attach it to the bodice. Before it dries, sculpt the piece so that it shapes around the bust.

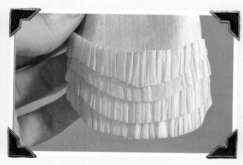

8. Attach your skirt ruffles using your paintbrush and craft glue. Place the largest ruffle first (#1), lining its bottom with the bottom of the skirt. Glue ruffle #2, followed by #3, then #4, lining each up with the *top* of the previous ruffle.

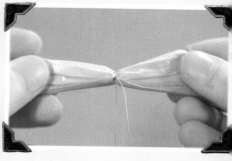

9. Cut a 3.5" x 3.5" piece of iridescent white tissue paper. Loosely pleat the tissue paper and tie a piece of thread at its center. It may be easier to loop the thread before slipping it over the tissue paper and tightening it.

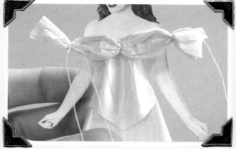

. Put a small dab of hot glue on e knot and attach it to the center the bust.

11. At each shoulder, use your thread to tie another knot. Fuss with the tissue paper a bit to retain some volume and nicely defined folds.

12. Drape the ends of the tissue paper around the shoulders and fix them into place with hot glue applied to the back of the doll's shoulders. Trim any hanging threads.

. Create the first drape of the irt by pleating a 5" x 3" piece of idescent tissue paper (lengthwise ft to right) and tying a knot one- ird from its right end.

14. Put a dab of hot glue on the knot, attaching it to the skirt, slightly off center and just above the ruffles.

15. Shape the tissue paper so that it curves around the skirt. *Don't stress about each individual fold!* Think big picture. Once you are satisfied with the drape, glue the tissue paper ends to the reverse of the skirt with hot glue.

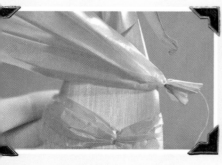

6. Repeat step 13 to create a sec- nd drape for the skirt. Put a small ab of hot glue on the knot and ttach it to the edge of the dress, bout halfway between the top of e first drape and the bottom edge f the bodice.

17. Drape this second piece of tissue paper to your satisfaction, securing its ends to the reverse of the skirt with hot glue.

18. Now you've created the dress and it's time to embellish it with Reo's wedding roses!

Family Parlor Reo

Reo's Wedding Dress Bouquet

1. These white roses from The Paper Studio® are the perfect touch for Reo's wedding gown.

2. Disassemble the first rose into several smaller blooms. Flatten the larger blooms so that they will not protrude too much from the dress.

3. Use white, red, and yellow acrylic paint to create a peach color. Don't mix the paint; instead, use a fine brush to lightly dab the different colors in layers on the flower petals.

4. Choose some tiny floral elements to add greenery to your design.

5. Attach the painted rose blooms to the tiny green leaves with a touch of hot glue.

6. Attach a piece of greenery to the skirt to serve as a guide for the placement of your roses. Repeat steps 2–5 to cover the skirt.

Family Parlor Lucille

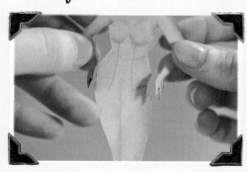

1. When draping onto the photocopy of your Lucille doll, snip the hands away from the body, as pictured on the left. Repeat steps 1-6 of Reo's Family Parlor tutorial to create Lucille's bodice and skirt.

2. Accordion pleat the two train pieces.

3. Use hot glue to attach the pleated train pieces to the back of Lucille's skirt.

4. Take one of the tiny daisies apart and snip its petals open on one side; repeat. These will be Lucille's sleeves. Before you attach them with hot glue, determine how they will drape around her shoulders.

Cut a tiny triangle of pale blue tissue paper. Use the pattern piece for Reo's bodice insert. Attach the tissue paper piece to the bodice using craft glue and a paintbrush.

6. Choose a lace for the bodice and determine how much you will need by draping it. Delicate laces with fine detail will work best. Note that the lace only has to reach the waist, which will be covered.

7. Glue the lace in place with craft glue and a paintbrush, trimming as you go. Repeat this for the other side of the bodice. Try to use the bodice lace in a way that connects it nicely to the dress sleeves.

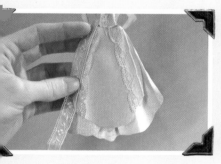

When choosing lace for the skirt, you'll want a slightly larger pattern than the bodice lace. The skirt has two lace fragments layered on top of each other. The top lace has a flower pattern, to be painted later.

9. The lace in Lucille's dress is a fabulous opportunity to repurpose a bit of tattered Victorian lace! Spend some time playing with different options until you are satisfied with your arrangement.

10. Cut some more of the tissue paper from step 5 into a 4.5" x 1.5" piece. Fold this piece so that it is about .25" wide (retaining its 4.5" length) and wrap it around the waist, meeting in an "x."

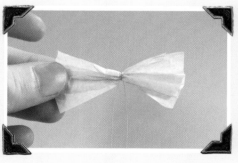

1. Glue the tissue paper sash in place and snip the ends to the waist.

12. Tie embroidery thread around the center of a 1.5" x 1.5" piece of pleated blue tissue paper. Dab hot glue on the knot to attach to the waist. Snip it to a pleasing length.

13. Use a paintbrush to paint a bit of color into the flowers on the skirt lace, mimicking embroidery. You can tone down the color by painting over it with pearl white paint.

Canvas City

EQUIPMENT

hot glue gun
hot glue sticks
craft glue
glue stick
paintbrush
acrylic paint
paper doll duplicates
Canvas City templates

Step right up and perform your own feats of crafting gymnastics! Join the greatest little show on Earth, where paper defies its singular dimension!

The circus has remained a beloved fixture of American culture since the late eighteenth century. The first complete circus performed for a season in Philadelphia, with George Washington in attendance! Numerous circus troupes and theaters eventually emerged, displaying the extraordinary talents of both human and animal performers.

When Reo and Lucille skipped town, they traded in their designer gowns for garments that allowed a freer range of movement. Inspired by the color and life of the circus, their costumes recall its golden days. Let circus posters and photographs from the late 1800s inspire your creations!

MATERIALS: REO

1. gold paper doily
2. yellow thread
3. iridescent peach paper
4. pale blue paper
5. blue and yellow tissue paper
6. adhesive gemstones
7. small blue feather
8. yellow rick rack
9. gold velvet ribbon
10. orange velvet flower petals
11. gold paper scraps

MATERIALS: LUCILLE

1. purple velvet ribbon
2. The Paper Studio® Silver Trim Border
3. pale pink ostrich feather
4. The Paper Studio® Silver Vellum Paper
5. silk flower petals (pink + purple.
6. Recollections® Raspberry Glitter Paper
7. orange, blue, and yellow tissue paper scraps
8. The Paper Studio® Multi Color Gemstones
9. pale blue paper
Shimmering Silver DecoA [not shown]
Dazzling Metallics Paint lavender tissue paper [not shown]

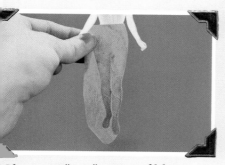

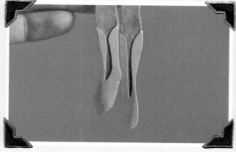

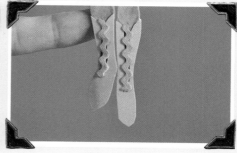

Glue a 4.5" x 2" piece of blue tissue paper to Reo's legs with a glue stick. Once the tissue paper has been smoothed across her legs, trim away the excess, leaving the shape of her legs.

2. Use craft glue to glue the shoe pieces to Reo's feet. After they have dried to a point where they are secure, trim away the excess paper, leaving the shape of her feet.

3. Drape the yellow rick rack across the shoes, cutting pieces (a bit less than one inch) that cover from the ankle to the top of the boot. Attach the rick rack to the boots using craft glue and a paintbrush.

Cut a rectangular 3.5" x 3.5" piece of yellow tissue paper. Pleat and tie a piece of thread in the center to mimic gathering.

5. Put a dab of hot glue on the knot and attach it to the doll.

6. Drape the tissue paper so that it wraps around Reo's hips and fix both sides to the back of the doll form with hot glue.

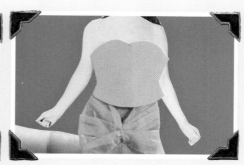

Pleat a 7" by 3" piece of the same tissue paper used in step 4. Cut it in half and fan the pieces.

8. Use hot glue to fix the two pieces to the back of the paper doll.

9. Run a thin line of glue down the edge of the doll's right abdomen. Glue the bodice so that its edge lines up with the doll. The other side of the bodice should now hang over the doll's left abdomen.

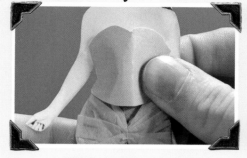

10. Push the unglued edge of the bodice towards the center of the doll's abdomen and secure it with hot glue. This should cause the bodice piece to buckle out in the middle.

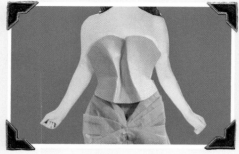

11. Point your hot glue gun into the cleavage; apply a generous amount of glue. Before it cools, push the bodice into the glue, creating two ridges. You can snip any excess bodice paper to keep it trim.

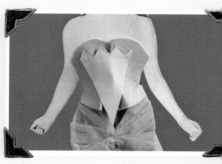

12. Use the template to create Reo' bodice insert from the reverse of your gold doily or bit of lace. Appl craft glue to the bodice insert with a paintbrush and attach it to the bodice, sculpting it to fit the bust.

13. Create Reo's cincher by draping velvet flower petals onto her bodice or by using the template provided. The ideal material can be sculpted cleanly around the bust. Velvet ribbon would also work nicely.

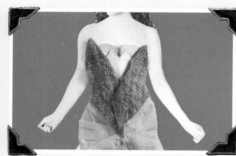

14. If you are using flower petals or cut-velvet ribbon, repeat the drape on both sides of the bodice, alternately gluing and trimming any excess fabric to keep the lines of her abdomen trim.

15. Snip some flourishes from you gold doily and use a paintbrush a craft glue to fix them onto Reo's cincher.

Circus Accessories to Dazzle and Delight

16. Cut a V-shaped piece of gold paper. Use your paintbrush and craft glue to fix it onto Reo's head, as shown.

17. Once the headband glue has dried, embellish it with an adhesive gemstone.

18. Use a dab of hot glue to fix a feather to the back of Reo's head.

19. Create Reo's armbands with tiny rectangular morsels of gold paper. Glue them to the arms using a paintbrush and craft glue. You may find it helpful to cut them to a satisfactory width, but leave them long when gluing them to the doll. Once the glue has dried, you can cut them flush with Reo's arms.

Glue a 4.5" x 2" piece of lavender tissue paper to Lucille's legs with a glue stick. Once the tissue paper has been smoothed across her legs, trim away the excess, leaving the shape of her legs.

2. Repeat steps 9-11 of Reo's Canvas City tutorial to create Lucille's bodice.

3. Lightly brush glue onto the belt piece with your paintbrush. Attach the belt to the bodice, with the pointed end of the star lined up between the bust.

Accordion pleat the four skirt pieces.

5. Attach the largest skirt piece (skirt piece #1) to Lucille's waist, using your hot glue.

6. Attach skirt piece #2 opposite skirt piece #1. Once both pieces are in place, finish the skirt by layering pieces #3 and #4 on top. Trim away at waist if it seems too full.

Arrange your silver trim across the front of the skirt so that it hides any hot glue or odd edges. If the trim is not adhesive, glue it to Lucille's waist with craft glue.

8. Pull the metallic ribbon so that it wraps tightly around Lucille's waist. Use hot glue to secure it to the back of the doll. Trim down the ends.

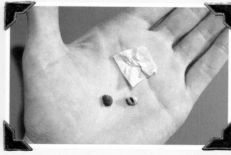

9. Create three "pompoms" by crumpling tiny squares of brightly colored tissue paper into little balls.

10. Attach your "pompoms" in a neat little row down the front of Lucille's bodice, using your paintbrush to apply craft glue.

11. Use a finely tipped paintbrush to add a subtle border of silver paint to the top of Lucille's bodice.

12. Create the straps from little snips of your purple velvet ribbon. Attach these with a paintbrush and craft glue.

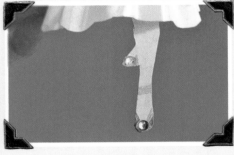

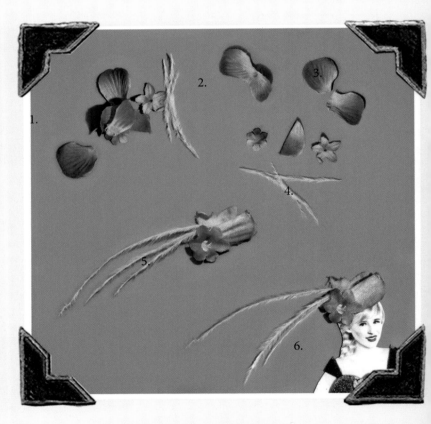

13. Trace the outline of Lucille's shoes with a pencil and then use a finely tipped paintbrush to apply mustard-colored paint. When the paint has dried, tiny gemstone embellishments add a nice sparkle.

Belle-of-the-Circus Hat

1. It only takes a few colorful scraps to create Lucille's show-stopping hat! Gather your silk flowers and pink ostrich feather for this circus millinery.

2. Pick a flower with petals that are 1-1.5" long. Disassemble it and choose a petal for the base of your hat.

3. Snip your chosen petal in half, or trim it so that it is a little longer than the width of Lucille's head. Holding it to the doll's head will help you to determine its size and suitability.

4. Fold the petal in half and secure it with a bit of hot glue. Snip a few 1.75–2" strands from the feather. Pick two smaller petals to accent your base petal.

5. Hot glue the smaller petals to the back and front of the hat. Glue the ostrich feathers in place.

6. Set your hat at a jaunty angle using nonpermanent adhesive!

Cotton Blossom

EQUIPMENT

hot glue gun
hot glue sticks
craft glue
scissors
paintbrush
paper doll duplicates
decorative scissors
Cotton Blossom templates

Play make-believe with the sisters aboard the nation's dandiest showboat!

The story of the American showboat is a chapter in frontier history. From the 1830s to the 1940s, these floating theaters rolled down American waterways bringing color, music, and drama to remote river towns and enchanting audiences against the backdrop of the mysterious Mississippi.

Edna Ferber immortalized both the romance and the tribulations of life aboard a turn-of-the-century showboat in her novel *Show Boat,* which became a celebrated musical. Sing along as you create your own colorful costumes!

MATERIALS: REO

Celebrate It® Luxe Wired Edge Velvet Ribbon (royal blue)
lavender tissue paper
scrap of orange velvet ribbon
The Paper Studio® Crinkle White Paper (use reverse side.)
yellow construction paper

6. purple flower petal
7. The Paper Studio® Tiny Stripe Yellow/White Paper
8. The Paper Studio® mini pearl alphabet adhesives
9. white feather
10. white/cream lace
Purple thread [not shown]

MATERIALS: LUCILLE

1. mint tissue paper
2. blue feather
3. pink feather
4. The Paper Studio® Crepe-White Paper
5. pale purple-colored flower petal
6. mint paper
7. Recollections® Blue Damask Scrapbook Paper

8. striped paper
9. peach-colored flower petal
10. berry-colored cardstock
11. The Paper Studio® mini pearl alphabet adhesives
12. white/cream lace
FolkArt® Pearl White Metallic Acrylic Paint [not shown]

1. Run a thin line of hot glue down Reo's right abdomen. Place the shirt piece so that its edge lines up with the right side of her body.

2. Push the unglued edge of the shirt towards the center of the doll's abdomen and secure it with hot glue. This should cause the bodice piece to buckle out in the middle.

3. Point your hot glue gun up into the bottom of Reo's shirt, applying bit of glue. Before it cools, push th middle of the shirt into the glue, creating some blousy dimension.

4. Glue the shirt to the doll at the shoulders and snip any excess shirt paper at the waist, keeping Reo's figure trim.

5. Determine the placement of Reo's shirt lace by draping it onto her, and snipping it how you please. In the original, the lace runs from the top of her shoulder to her waist.

6. Repeat for the opposite side of Reo's shirt, and use craft glue and paintbrush to attach the lace piece

7. After gluing the lace to Reo's shirt front, you can use a second type of lace for her cuffs. Cut a piece slightly longer than the cuff's width. Glue it to the cuff with craft glue, wrapping its ends around Reo's elbows.

8. Repeat for Reo's second sleeve.

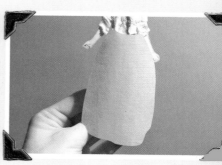

9. Gently flex Reo's skirt piece to give it a bit of dimension. Run you hot glue along the edge of her righ hip and place the skirt so that its edge lines up with the edge of the doll.

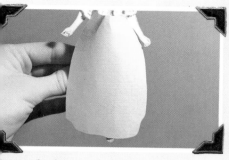

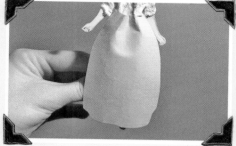

0. Push the unglued edge of the skirt towards the center of the doll; the skirt will protrude in the front. Fix the unglued side of the skirt into place with hot glue—its edges should line up with the body edge.

11. Point your hot glue gun down into the front of the skirt, applying a small amount of glue. Before it cools, push the top of the skirt into the glue, creating two "pleats" in the top of the skirt.

12. Pleat a 5" by 7.5" piece of lavender tissue paper (lengthwise left to right). Tie a piece of thread around the tissue paper, about one-third from the right end.

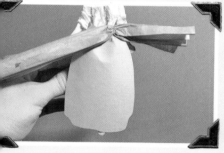

. Put a dab of hot glue on the thread knot and attach it to Reo's skirt waist, slightly off center.

14. Work the tissue paper so that it drapes around the sides of the skirt. If you have trouble covering the desired area with the single tissue paper drape, you can always layer a second over it.

15. Trim the tissue paper so that it is slightly longer than the yellow skirt piece.

. Fold the tissue paper around the yellow skirt and fix it in place with hot glue. Cut a curve-shaped piece of royal blue velvet ribbon and attach it to Reo's waist with craft glue. Wrap and glue its ends to the reverse of the doll.

17. Create a slight rippling fold in Reo's larger cravat piece before gluing it to the top of the smaller C-shaped cravat piece. You may want to trim the pieces down so that their proportion works better with the blouse.

18. To create Reo's hat, fold a silk flower petal around her head and fix it in place with hot glue. Embellish the petal with a snippet of feather and velvet ribbon. (See page 87 for more hat inspiration.)

1. Glue a scrap of crepe-white paper to Lucille's chest. You may want to slightly round the top edge so that it follows the shape of her chin. You'll only see a bit of this peeking out of her jacket, so no need to get too fussy.

2. Gently flex Lucille's skirt piece to give it a bit of dimension. Remember that, for your Lucille How-tos, snipping her hands away from her body will always make it easier to sculpt around the hips.

3. Follow steps 9-10 of Reo's Cotton Blossom How-To to attach Lucille's skirt to her body.

4. Point your hot glue gun down into the front of Lucille's skirt, applying a small amount of glue. Before it cools, push the top of the skirt into the glue, creating two "pleats" in the top of the skirt.

5. Attach Lucille's jacket by following steps 1-2 of Reo's Cotton Blossom How-To. Keep Lucille's midsection shapely by trimming any extra jacket paper hanging off the edges of her body.

6. Point your hot glue gun up into the bottom of Reo's jacket, applying a bit of glue. Before it cools, push the middle of the jacket into the glue, creating two ridges. Glue the jacket to the doll at its shoulders.

7. Cut a 4.5" by 5" piece of mint tissue paper.

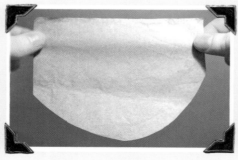

8. Use your scissors to round one of the long sides of the tissue paper.

9. Begin pleating the tissue paper at the opposite end of its rounded edge.

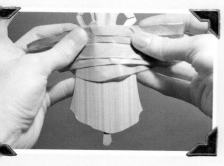

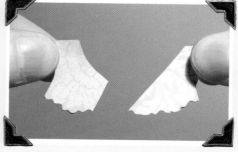

. Fan the pleats so that the tissue per is about half the length of the rt. Place the tissue paper piece so at its top edge lines up with the ist with its rounded edge on the ttom.

11. Fold the piece of pleated tissue paper around the skirt and glue its ends to the back of the doll.

12. For an optional detail, use your fancy scissors to embellish the bottom of the two bodice pieces. The pattern pieces include a bit of allowance so that they will not end up too short.

. Using craft glue and a paint-ush, attach the first bodice piece the jacket on Lucille's right side.

14. Using craft glue and a paint-brush, attach the second bodice piece to Lucille's left side.

15. Determine the placement of Lucille's jacket lace by draping it on her, and snipping it how you please. In the original, the lace runs from her shoulder to about her belly button.

. Use craft glue and a paintbrush attach the first piece of lace to cille's jacket. You may want to ip Lucille's hair from her shoulder, order to tuck the top of the lace tween her hair and shoulder.

17. Repeat for the opposite side of Lucille's jacket.

18. From your laces, determine a good snippet that you can use as a border on Lucille's skirt drapery. Cut it a little longer than you think you will need.

19. Using craft glue and a paint-brush, attach the lace to the bottom of the tissue paper drapery, folding its ends around the skirt and securing them to its reverse.

20. Glue a thin bit of white trim to the cuffs of Lucille's sleeves, wrapping their ends around her elbows.

21. Add three tiny pearl buttons to the blue bodice piece on Lucille's jacket and one pearl to the cuffs of each sleeves. Glue the bow-tie piece to the neckline, and add a tiny square piece from the same paper to finish it off.

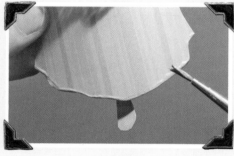

22. Use a finely tipped paintbrush to add a border of pearl-white metallic paint to the skirt hem.

Lucille's Jaunty Traveling Cap

1. With a few crafting scraps, you can create Lucille's lovely traveling hat! You'll need two kinds of silk flowers and two contrasting feathers for this showboat millinery.

2. Snip a petal to slightly larger than the width of Lucille's head; this will be the hat base. Cut a tiny triangular piece from your second flower petal and trim a few strands of your blue feather.

3. Fold the larger petal piece into itself, putting a dab of hot glue in the fold, and catching the feather and triangular snippet in the glue.

4. Glue the second feather piece to the back of the hat, trimming any excess off of its bottom.

5. Position the hat onto Lucille's head at a jaunty angle. Now you're ready to sail the Mississippi!

New Orleans

EQUIPMENT

hot glue gun
hot glue sticks
craft glue
scissors
paintbrush
acrylic paint
paper doll duplicates
New Orleans templates

Dance your way down to the Big Easy and "laissez les bon temps rouler!" New Orleans is known as the birthplace of jazz and beignets, and the playground of pirates and voodoo queens. It's also known for a lively little celebration called Mardi Gras. . . .

To the outside world, Mardi Gras may stir up images of rowdy spring breakers, flashing—ahem—what their mamas gave 'em in exchange for a bead or two. The true Mardi Gras celebration has more history and soul—it was celebrated in New Orleans as early as the 1730s, when the city's leaders established elegant society balls, a practice still very much alive today.

Lucille and Reo are decked out in the official colors of the season: purple, green, and gold. According to tradition, purple stands for justice; gold for power; and green for faith.

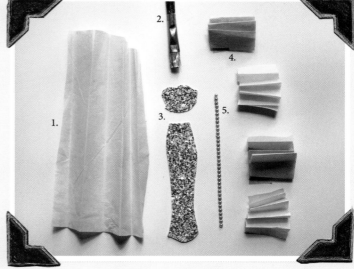

MATERIALS: REO

1. Martha Stewart Crafts® Twilight Blue Pearl Acrylic Paint
2. Sharpie® Metallic Fine Point Bronze Marker
3. Recollections® Glitter Cardstock (lavender)
4. The Paper Studio® Crinkle Copper Paper
5. The Paper Studio® Silver Vellum Paper
6. gold star nail decal
7. purple tissue paper
8. gold upholstery trim
FolkArt® Metallics Ice Blue Paint [not shown]

MATERIALS: LUCILLE

1. yellow tissue paper
2. FolkArt® Metallics Ice Blue Paint
3. Recollections® Glitter Cardstock (multicolor)
4. lavender tissue paper
5. The Paper Studio® Pearl Gemstones

1. Pleat the four pieces of Reo's skirt.

2. Use hot glue to attach the two larger skirt sections to Reo's waist, as shown.

3. Attach the two remaining skirt pieces to Reo's waist with hot glue. If you find that you want more fullness in the skirt, you can always cut and add another piece or two!

4. Using a medium/large soft-bristle paintbrush, cover the skirt with a *thin* layer of the twilight blue pearl paint. Long, quick sweeps of the paintbrush will keep the paint from getting streaky.

5. Fold a 2"-long piece of purple tissue paper so that it is .25" wide. Glue this at an angle to Reo's bust.

6. Fold a second 2"-long piece of the purple tissue paper so that it is .25" wide. Glue this at an angle to the opposite side of her bust. Trim the ends of the pieces so that they are flush with Reo's shoulders.

7. Before you attach the bodice, flex it to give it a bit of rounded dimension. Apply hot glue to the edges of Reo's abdomen and attach the bodice, lining up its edges with the edges of Reo's body.

8. Point your hot glue gun into the cleavage of Reo's bodice, applying a fair amount of hot glue. Before it cools, push the middle of the bodice into the glue, creating two ridges.

9. Trim any excess bodice paper hanging over the edges of the body. Glue the belt so that its point is between Reo's bust. Wrap the ends of the belt around the body and fix them to the back of the doll with hot glue.

0. Use a paintbrush and craft glue o place your star nail decal on Reo's eckline. Draw its chain with your opper Sharpie. Hold your chosen ollar embellishment to the doll to etermine how much you will need.

11. Snip the embellishment to your chosen length and use as much hot glue as you need to secure it to the back of Reo's shoulders.

12. Create Reo's gloves by applying a thin layer of the ice-blue paint to her forearms and hands, starting at the elbow.

Before you attach Lucille's skirt iece, flex it to give it a bit of ounded dimension.

2. Run your hot glue down the inner edges of the skirt piece and center it onto Lucille's body.

3. Before you attach the bodice, flex it to give it a bit of rounded dimension.

Use hot glue applied to the edges f Lucille's abdomen to attach the odice, lining up its edges with the dges of Lucille's body.

5. Point your hot glue gun into the cleavage of Lucille's bodice, applying a fair amount of hot glue. Before it cools, push the middle of the bodice into the glue, creating two ridges.

6. Pleat a 3.5" x 10" piece of yellow tissue paper (lengthwise left to right) so that it is about 1.25" wide (10" long) before cutting it in half.

7. Snip Lucille's hands away from her hips. Tuck her lower body into the folds of the tissue paper so that the top of the pleated tissue paper lines up with her waist.

8. Fold the top corner of the tissue paper around her body so that it hugs the hips, creating a nice curve. Glue this fold to the reverse of her body. Trim the bottom of the pleated paper so that it is even with the rest of the skirt.

9. Repeat steps 6-9 for the opposite side of the dress.

10. Cut a 1.5" by 2" piece of the yellow tissue paper. Slice into one side of it to create a diagonal line.

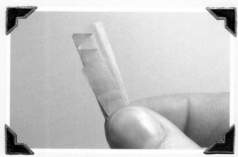

11. Pleat the piece of tissue paper and fan it slightly.

12. Place your fanned piece of tissue paper into the top of the bodice and determine how long you want it to be. Snip it to your desired length and use hot glue to secure it into place.

13. Repeat steps 10-11 with a piece of lavender tissue paper. Glue this to Lucille's back shoulder.

14. Repeat steps 10-13 to complete Lucille's ruffled collar, reversing the colors on the second side.

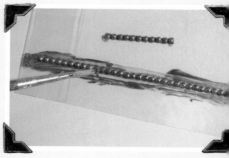

15. Paint your adhesive pearls in green, purple, and gold acrylic pai to transform them into Mardi Gra beads. Affix them to your reveling dolls!

Western Skies

EQUIPMENT

hot glue gun
hot glue sticks
craft glue
scissors
paintbrush
acrylic paint
paper doll duplicates
Western Skies templates

Go West, young lady!

Though life on the American frontier was not always as glamorous as its portrayal in the Western shows, female superstars like "Little Sure Shot" Annie Oakley were enormously influential in creating its mythology—and that of the cowgirl. Women's successes paved the way for suffragists and women's rights activists. Famous for their pony and gun tricks, many of the best-loved cowgals were also conservationists, philanthropists, and—in the case of Lillian Smith, reportedly—shameless flirts.

By adopting or modifying menswear, ladies' Western wear combines function with style. Hats off to May Lillie, Lulu Bell Parr, Ruth Roach Salmon, and Vera McGinnis—inspirations for your creations!

MATERIALS: REO

sheer white or cream ribbon
brown paper
gold floral pattern paper
artisanal-pressed pink paper
The Paper Studio® Tea Stained Leather Paper
wrapping paper scrap with gold detail
ale blue ribbon [not shown]
quid Pearls™ Silver Dimensional Pearlescent Paint [not own]

MATERIALS: LUCILLE

1. pale blue ribbon
2. artisan-pressed white cotton paper
3. The Paper Studio® Tiny Stripe Green/White Paper
4. Decorative Specialty Paper Seersucker Stripe Fern
5. green cardstock
6. Ideal Home Range cocktail napkin

7. The Paper Studio® Leather Paper
8. The Paper Studio® Crinkle Bronze Paper (use reverse.
9. wrapping paper scrap with gold detail

Liquid Pearls™ Silver [not shown]

Dimensional Pearlescent Paint [not shown]

1. To create Reo's cowgirl boots, first use a paintbrush to cover her legs in craft glue. Cut a 1.75" x 4"piece of the tea-stained leather paper and place it on her legs. Trim it to the shape of her legs.

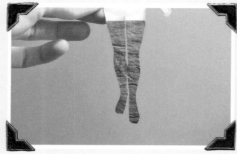

2. Once you have trimmed the leather paper to the shape of Reo's legs, you may want to embellish it to look more like boots. A Sharpie or acrylic paint will help to add detail like shoelaces or leather stitching.

3. Make a thin line of hot glue dov the edge of Reo's right abdomen. Place the corresponding shirt bod piece so that its outer edge lines u with the edge of the doll.

4. Push the unglued side of the shirt bodice piece towards the center line of the doll's abdomen and fix it into place with hot glue.

5. Repeat steps 3-4 for the second shirt bodice piece.

6. Flex the sleeve pieces so that they are slightly rounded.

7. Using hot glue, attach the two sleeve pieces. You may fold any excess sleeve paper over the arm, or trim it down as desired.

8. From your ribbon, cut a .25"-wide piece that will work as trim for the skirt.

9. Use craft glue and a paintbrush to attach the shirt trim to the overlapping shirt bodice piece. Us the same ribbon to embellish Reo shirt cuffs.

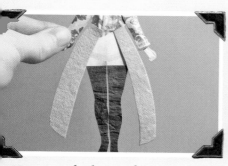

. Using craft glue and a intbrush, glue the two narrower irt pieces to Reo's hips. Craft glue ll allow you to adjust them when u place the third skirt piece, if cessary.

11. Glue the larger skirt piece to Reo's waist with craft glue so that it is slightly overlapping the other two skirt pieces. If necessary, adjust the two side skirt pieces so that there are no gaps. Make sure that the waistlines of the three skirt pieces line up.

12. Use the same ribbon you used for the blouse as a border on the skirt. Apply a thin amount of craft glue to the bottom of the larger skirt piece where you want to place it. Place the ribbon and trim its ends flush with the skirt.

. Apply and trim this border to e side pieces of the skirt using the me method as step 12. Tuck the bbons' inner ends under the center irt piece. Trim the outer ends of e ribbon to be flush with the skirt.

14. Wrap your pale blue ribbon around Reo's waist. Use craft glue to attach it in the front of the skirt, and use hot glue to attach its ends to the reverse of the skirt.

15. Create a miniature belt buckle by cutting a .25" three-sided square from gold paper. In this case, a scrap of gold-embellished wrapping paper worked nicely, though any gold paper will do.

. Use your paintbrush to apply small amount of craft glue to the verse of the "belt buckle." Attach it the ribbon "belt," in the middle of :o's waist. Add the blouse and cuff ttons with dimensional paint.

17. Cut a slit in your hat piece, slightly off center. You want to create a slit that is wide enough to slip over Reo's head, but not so wide that it will slip past her face.

18. Place the hat piece on Reo's head and secure it with your paintbrush and craft glue. Roll the front slightly down and forward to give it some dimension. Bend the back of the hat so that it curves slightly upward.

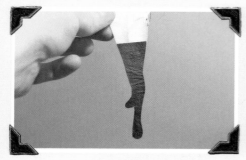

1. Repeat steps 1-2 of Reo's Western Skies How-To to create Lucille's boots.

2. Repeat steps 3-7 of Reo's Western Skies How-To to create Lucille's blouse.

3. Using craft glue and a paint-brush, attach .25"-wide snippets of the shirt paper to Lucille's wrists. Trim them down to create cuffs.

4. Use sharp scissors to create the fringe on your three skirt fringe pieces.

5. Attach the three pieces of fringe to their corresponding skirt pieces using craft glue.

6. Using craft glue and a paint-brush, glue the two narrower skirt pieces to Lucille's hips. Craft glue will allow you to adjust them when you place the third skirt piece, if necessary.

7. Glue the larger skirt piece to Lucille's waist with craft glue to slightly overlap the other two skirt pieces. Adjust the two side pieces so that there are no gaps. Make sure that the three waistlines line up.

8. From your cocktail napkin, cut a 2" x 2" square.

9. Make a diagonal cut through your small square napkin piece.

). Overlap the two napkin pieces so that their patterns are both cing in the same direction and eir wider points are slightly at of alignment. Glue the pieces gether in this fashion with a mall amount of craft glue.

11. Trim the napkin piece in half so that its size as a handkerchief is more realistic relative to the doll's body. Use craft glue to attach the napkin "handkerchief" to Lucille, hanging it just over her bust.

12. Wrap the ends of the "handkerchief" around her shoulders and glue them in place on the reverse of the doll. Cut and glue two small snippets of napkin to the back of one of Lucille's shoulders to mimic a knot.

3. Cut a thin, parenthesis-shaped iver of tan leather paper and use raft glue to attach it as Lucille's elt. If the piece is longer than the aist, wrap its ends around the doll nd glue them to her backside.

14. Cut a tiny piece from your wrapping paper scrap (or similarly patterned paper) and attach it as Lucille's belt buckle. You can also substitute something like Reo's belt (Reo: *Western Skies,* step 15).

15. Use craft glue to attach your pale blue ribbon to the base of your hat.

6. Use craft glue to attach the rim of Lucille's hat to her head, rapping it so that it protrudes ightly.

17. Glue the ribbon-festooned hat piece from step 15 to Lucille's head, placing it behind the brim.

18. Trim the body of the hat down to better fit the shape of Lucille's head. Cut a subtle dip in its center to mimic a true Stetson. Add tiny blouse and cuff buttons with your dimensional paint.

Dreamland

EQUIPMENT

hot glue gun
hot glue sticks
craft glue
scissors
paintbrush
acrylic paint
paper doll duplicates
Dreamland templates

Swim in a city of live mermaids under the glow of 1,000,000 twinkling lights!

The tale of New York City's Dreamland amusement park is stranger than fiction. Though its existence was short-lived, its stories and characters are now a beloved part of Coney Island's colorful mythology.

To inspire your own mermaid tails, look to bewitching antique illustrations of mermaids and study the scales of tropical fish. And be sure to take a peek at an old diving suit or two; Reo must have been extraordinarily brave to strap herself into such a contraption!

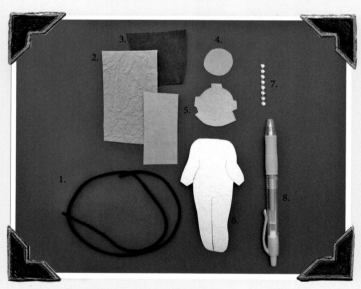

MATERIALS: REO

1. black nylon decorative trim cord
2. The Paper Studio® Leather Paper
3. black cardstock paper
4. blue vellum or semi-transparent blue paper
5. iridescent copper paper
6. cream-colored paper with canvas texture
7. The Paper Studio® Round Gray Gemstones
8. Pilot Gold Ink Gel Pen
Liquid Pearls™ Silver Dimensional Pearlescent Paint
FolkArt® Pearl White Metallic Acrylic Paint
Sharpie® Fine Point Permanent Marker [last three items not shown]

MATERIALS: LUCILLE

1. gold metallic skeleton leaves
2. paper with scale texture
3. The Paper Studio® Newsprint Microflowers
4. The Paper Studio® Gemstones Ivory Chevron
5. silk flower petal
6. The Paper Studio® Silver Vellum Paper
7. The Paper Studio® Gemstones Small Pearl Flourish
8. gold doily
FolkArt® Pearl White Metallic Acrylic Paint [not shown]
DecoArt Dazzling Metallics Venetian Gold Acrylic Paint [not shown]

1. Run a thin line of hot glue along the edge of the diving suit's inner arm. Fix the arm into place behind the suit's hip in such a way that the front midsection of the suit protrudes slightly.

2. Repeat step 1 for the second arm of the suit. When you are finished, your piece should have subtle dimension.

3. Attach the diving suit to Reo, running craft glue along her legs and arms and avoiding her mid-section. The bottom of the leg cuffs should line up with her ankles. The suit will ride high and large on her shoulders.

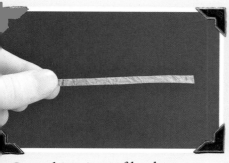

4. Cut a thin piece of leather textured paper, 2.5" long and one-eighth-inch wide. This will become the belt.

5. Using a paintbrush, apply craft glue to a little less than half the length of your strip of leather paper. Place it at Reo's waist, lining up its edge with the edge of the suit.

6. Snip the excess leather paper hanging over the waist so that its edge is flush with the doll's edge .

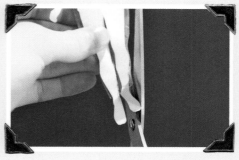

7. Take the snipped piece of leather paper from step 6 and use craft glue to fix it over the first leather paper strip. Manipulate the piece so that there is a slight ripple in its center where the belt buckle would be. Trim the long edge to a point.

8. Using the same leather paper that you used for the belt, glue one-eighth-inch-wide cuffs to the diving suit. You may want to use pieces that are longer than the sleeves are wide and then trim them down.

9. Use scissors to shape the legs of the diving suit to Reo's calves.

10. Cut a 1.5" x 1.5" piece of leather paper and use craft glue to attach it slightly below the doll's knees.

11. Trim around the leather paper, revealing the shape of Reo's feet.

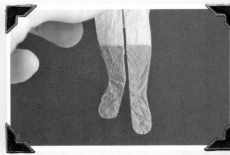

12. Use your scissors to shape the leather paper around the feet so that it looks like two distinct boots.

13. Glue one-sixteenth-inch-wide pieces of leather paper to the boots for straps. Use a gold gel pen or colored pencil to add detail.

14. Cut a small square of your black cardstock, making sure that it is at least as wide as your helmet piece. Attach it to the back of your helmet with craft glue.

15. Trim the black cardstock so that it forms a border at the base of the helmet.

16. Cut Reo's head off at the shoulders. Sorry, Reo! We'll reattach it after we get it "into" its helmet.

17. Using a paintbrush, cover Reo's face with a thin layer of glue. Either liquid craft glue or an Elmer's glue stick will work for this step.

18. Place the helmet "glass" onto Reo's face; center and smooth the paper into position. Instead of using paper for the "glass," cover Reo's face with Mod Podge® Dimensional Magic glue after the last step.

. Trim Reo's shoulders off, llowing the curve of the glass ece.

20. Use craft glue to attach the round glass piece with Reo's face to the helmet.

21. Use craft glue to attach the helmet to the shoulders of the diving suit.

. Add tiny notches to the belt ing your fine-tipped Sharpie pen.

23. Use dimensional paint to add a square belt buckle to the center of the belt where it ripples out.

24. Add a row of adhesive gray gemstones to the base of the helmet to simulate rivets. Use your gold gel pen to create line details on the helmet.

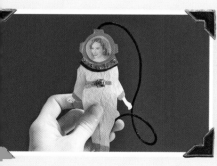

5. Cut your desired length from the lack nylon cord and attach it to the op of the helmet, using hot glue.

26. As a finishing touch, highlight the suit's dimension by lightly brushing over it with the pearl metallic paint.

1. Run a thin line of hot glue along the inner edge of the larger fin on Lucille's tail piece.

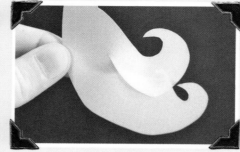

2. Pull the smaller fin forward and over the larger fin, gluing it into place. The tail should now protrude a bit where the two fins overlap.

3. Choose a gold metallic skeleton leaf whose curve works nicely with the shape of your tail fins. Cut it in half along the large center line.

4. Decide on the placement of the leaf piece on the front of the tail and attach it using craft glue.

5. Apply craft glue to the back of the leg piece's lower half and glue it to the tail's front.

6. Take another gold metallic skeleton leaf and cut it in half, this time *perpendicular* to the center vein. Use craft glue to fix it in place over Lucille's waist.

7. Use small scissors or an X-Acto blade to trim the metallic leaf at Lucille's waist and hips.

8. Use a paintbrush to cover Lucille with glue from her waist down, placing the tail so that it lines up with her waist and covers her feet.

9. Before placing Lucille's top, trim it down as desired. Glue it into place with craft glue.

. From your gold doily, cut a piece at will shape nicely to Lucille's uist.

11. Use craft glue to add your gold doily embellishment to the waist, wrapping any excess at its edges around her hips.

12. Attach the adhesive pearl flourishes to Lucille's top, trimming them down to the proper shape and size.

. If you are using newsprint icroflowers from The Paper udio, first remove the center mstone. Cut the remaining petal half.

14. Glue the two halves of your petal to the edge of Lucille's head. Repeat this step until her head is covered, cutting as many petals as you need.

15. Paint over the petal headpiece with pearl metallic paint.

. Once the paint has dried, bellish the headpiece with your hesive chevron gemstones.

17. Mix acrylic paint to create a color that is a slightly lighter hue than your scaley paper. Add gold or silver metallic paint and brush it onto the scales. Blot the paint with a paper towel, leaving a subtle sheen.

18. As a finishing touch, use hot glue to embellish the waist with a silk flower petal.

Explorers' Club

EQUIPMENT

hot glue gun
hot glue sticks
craft glue
scissors
paintbrush
acrylic paint
paper doll duplicates
Explorers' Club templates

Bundle up with the sisters as they race to the South Pole!

Reo and Lucille's friend Nina had many things in common with real-life journalist Nellie Bly. In a male-dominated world, Bly paved the way for female adventurers and professionals. After her undercover exploits in an infamous New York mental institution, she set out to beat Jules Verne's fictional *Around the World in 80 Days* record—and did. Though Bly never made it to the South Pole, her taste for adventure rivaled that of her famous male contemporaries, Amundsen and Scott.

The race to reach the South Pole captivated the world and pitted explorer against explorer. Amundsen emerged frozen and victorious in 1911, and it wasn't until 1969 that the first all-female expedition—a team from Ohio State University—reached the Pole. Many explorers of the "Heroic Age of Antarctic Exploration" used animal furs for warmth and protection against the elements of an unforgiving climate.

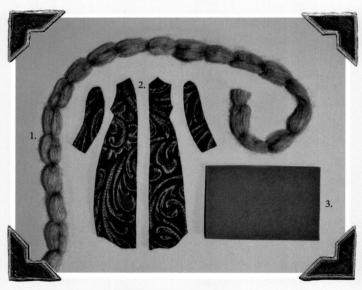

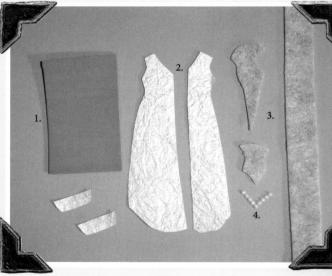

MATERIALS: REO

1. Patons® Cobbles™ Yarn Moon Rock
2. Creatology® Embossed Felt Galleria Cocoa
3. Creatology® Foam Sheet
Scrap of yellow ribbon [not shown]

MATERIALS: LUCILLE

1. Creatology® Foam Sheet
2. The Paper Studio® Crinkle Cream Paper
3. Creatology® Basic Felt Sandstone
4. The Paper Studio® Gemstones Ivory Chevron
   chunky white yarn
Scrap of mint ribbon [not shown]

Snip Reo's hair from her shoulders, d wrap a small piece of your scarf bon around her neck. Twist the bon in the front and secure it with a b of hot glue to Reo's chest. Trim the ds of the ribbon to above her waist.

2. Cut a piece of foam material to a rectangle whose width is about 1.5". Cover Reo's legs with a thin layer of craft glue and place the foam over them.

3. After the glue has dried a bit, trim the foam to the shape of Reo's legs.

Run a thin line of hot glue own the outer edge of Reo's left bdomen. Place the corresponding at piece.

5. Repeat step 4 for Reo's right side, overlapping the coat pieces slightly.

6. Snip excess coat material from the waist to keep Reo's figure trim.

Run a line of hot glue down each m and place the sleeves. Trim any cess sleeve material so that the idth of the sleeve is only slightly rger than that of the arm.

8. Tuck one end of the Moon Rock yarn under the left overlap of the coat. Glue it into place.

9. Run a line of hot glue along the edge of Reo's hair, shaping the yarn into the glue so that it frames her face as a hood.

10. Continue to hot glue the yarn in a continuous line down the edge of the overlapping coat piece. Follow the curve of the hem, wrapping the yarn to follow it, and finally trimming the yarn flush with the coat.

11. Finish the hem by gluing a small piece of yarn under the overlapping coat piece and trimming it to the edge of the coat. Two more snips of yarn glued to Reo's hands make matching mittens.

12. Cut a thin piece from the same material that you used for Reo's coat and wrap it around her waist, creating a belt. Hot glue its ends to the reverse of the doll.

Explorers' Club: Lucille

1. Snip Lucille's hair from her shoulders; wrap a small piece of mint ribbon around her neck. Twist the ribbon in front and fix it to her chest with a dab of hot glue. Trim the ribbon ends to above her waist.

2. Repeat steps 2-3 of Reo's Explorers' Club How-To to create Lucille's boots.

3. Run a thin line of hot glue down the outer edge of Lucille's left abdomen. Place the corresponding coat piece.

4. Repeat step 3 for Lucille's right side, overlapping the coat pieces slightly.

5. Before you place the sleeves, you may want to flex them to create a bit of dimension. Run a line of hot glue down each arm and attach the sleeve pieces.

6. Trim any excess sleeve material so that the width of the sleeve is only slightly larger than that of the arm.

Use craft glue and a paintbrush to ce Lucille's felt collar pieces. nipulate the pieces so that they ap slightly around Lucille's head. d .25"-wide snippets of the felt terial to her wrists, trimming m flush with her coat cuffs.

8. Cut a .75"-wide strip of the felt and glue it in two pieces to the hems of the skirt, tucking the one under the other. Trim the hem material down so that it is flush with the edges of the coat.

9. Glue the pocket pieces .75" below where Lucille's hands meet her hips. Glue them so that half hangs off the coat.

  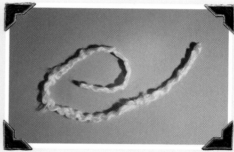

Fold the pocket pieces over and e the ends to the reverse of the at.

11. Add six adhesive gemstone buttons directly below where the bottom of the felt collar hits.

12. Select a scrap of chunky white or cream yarn that will match your coat. You won't need more than a foot's worth.

Cover the top of Lucille's head th hot glue and zigzag the yarn ck and forth across it.

14. When Lucille's head has been sufficiently covered against the chill, snip the end of the yarn.

High Flight

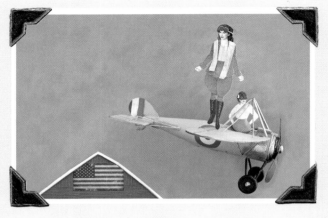

EQUIPMENT

Equipment:
hot glue gun
hot glue sticks
craft glue
scissors
paintbrush
acrylic paint
paper doll duplicates
High Flight templates

"Slip the surly bonds of Earth" and dance with the sisters across the sky!

Before modern safety regulations, aviation stunts were limited only by the pilot's bravery—or foolishness. Barnstorming reached its peak in the 1920s, after WWI, when the US government sold its surplus planes at a loss, making it an affordable hobby. Many of these early aviators—including a young Charles Lindbergh—traveled across the country, selling rides and performing stunts.

The prevalence of female and minority barnstormers challenged gender stereotypes and racism: African-American aviator Bessie Coleman used her influence to fight segregation. Daredevils won attention for such stunts as barrel rolls, staged crashes, dives, parachuting, and even playing tennis from the wings. Barnstormer Roscoe Turner developed his own original costume—and flew with a pet lion as his copilot! The lion, named Gilmore, was even outfitted with a special parachute.

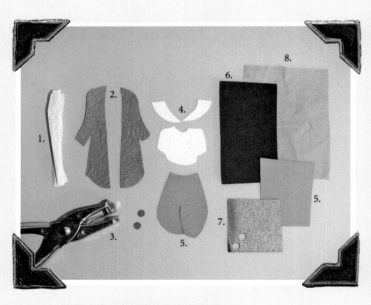

MATERIALS: REO

1. pale blue tissue paper
2. The Paper Studio® Leather Paper
3. hole punch
4. artisanal-pressed white cotton paper
5. taupe-colored paper
6. black paper
7. green iridescent paper
8. natural-colored tissue paper

MATERIALS: LUCILLE

1. black paper
2. brown paper
3. The Paper Studio® Tea Stained Leather Paper
4. The Paper Studio® Crinkle White Paper (use reverse).
5. taupe-colored paper
6. orange tissue paper
7. green iridescent paper
8. light-brown colored pencil

1. Make a thin line of hot glue down the edge of Reo's right abdomen. Place the corresponding shirt piece so that its outer edge lines up with the edge of the doll.

2. Push the unglued side of the shirt bodice piece towards the center line of the doll's abdomen and fix it into place with hot glue.

3. Repeat steps 1-2 for the left side of the shirt, and then add the collar, tucking its ends around the doll's neck.

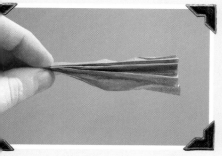

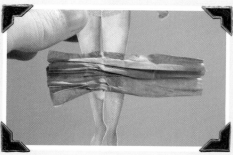

4. Loosely pleat a 2.5" x 2.5" piece taupe tissue paper.

5. Use your paintbrush to cover Reo's knees with craft glue, from the bottom of her thigh to the top of her calf. Place the pleated tissue paper across Reo's knees, pressing its folds into the glue.

6. Make a cut separating the tissue paper between the legs; trim its ends to .25" away from the outer edges of her legs. Wrap the ends of the tissue paper around her legs and secure them to the back with craft glue.

7. Use a paintbrush to cover your jodhpur piece with a thin layer of craft glue.

8. Glue the jodhpur piece to a rectangle of the same taupe tissue paper you used in steps 4-6.

9. Smooth out any wrinkles in the tissue paper and cut around the shape of the jodhpurs.

10. Run a thin line of hot glue along the inner edge of the left pant leg.

11. Pull the right leg so that it slightly crosses the left leg, fixing it into the hot glue.

12. Glue the jodhpurs to the doll, attaching them with hot glue at th hip and slightly above the knees.

13. Cut a 2" x 2" square of your black cardstock for Reo's boots. Cut into one side, creating a curved line.

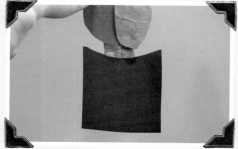

14. Using craft glue, place the piece of black cardstock over Reo's feet, with the curve of the paper hitting just below the knees.

15. Trim the black cardstock, following the shape of Reo's feet and calves. Use a gold gel pen or colored pencil to add shoelaces.

16. Glue the two coat pieces to Reo, attaching them by making lines of hot glue down her arms. Add .25"-wide paper cuffs to the sleeves.

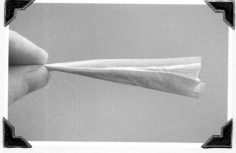

17. Pleat a 4.5" x 1" piece of pale blue tissue paper for Reo's scarf.

18. Use craft glue to position the pleated tissue paper over Reo's jacket, attempting to capture the natural drape of a scarf.

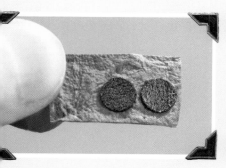

Using a regular paper hole
ch, punch out two circles from
r iridescent green cardstock.
e these to a small piece of
her-textured paper using craft
e.

20. Trim around the green circles, leaving a thin border of tan paper. Glue this piece to Reo's forehead, positioned over her eyes. Complete the illusion of goggles by adding a tiny snippet as a strap.

21. For a more fitted coat, trim excess material from the waist, arms, and shoulders. You may also want to shorten the length of the coat; rather than cutting a straight line at the hem, round its corners.

High Flight: Lucille

You have the option of creating
cille's blouse as one piece or
ipping it down the center and
peating steps 1-3 of Reo's High
ght How-To.

2. Run a thin line of hot glue down the inner edge of Lucille's right jodhpur leg.

3. Secure Lucille's right jodhpur leg to the back of the left jodhpur leg, bending the paper a bit so that it protrudes slightly.

Use your tan or light brown
ored pencil to add subtle
inkle lines to Lucille's jodhpurs.
u may want to shade the right leg
it, where the left leg overlaps it.

5. Use craft glue to attach a small piece of the black paper to Lucille's right foot.

6. Trim the black paper down so that it follows the shape of Lucille's right foot.

75

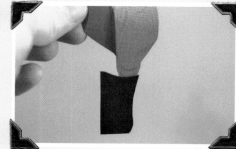

7. Cut another piece of the black paper and use your scissors to round one of its edges.

8. Use craft glue to attach the piece of black paper to Lucille's left calf, so that its curved edge is right below her knee.

9. Trim down the black paper so that it follows the shape of Lucille's foot. If desired, embellish as in step 15 of Reo's How-To.

10. Use craft glue to attach the helmet piece to Lucille's head. Trim it down to the shape of her head.

11. To create Lucille's goggles, repeat steps 19-21 of Reo's How-To.

12. Use a finely tipped paintbrush to add red, white, and blue embellishment to Lucille's leather helmet.

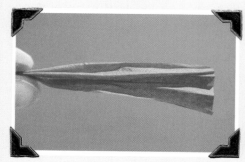

13. Loosely pleat a 2.5" piece of orange tissue paper.

14. Use craft glue to attach this orange "scarf" to Lucille's blouse.

Séance Parlor

EQUIPMENT

hot glue gun
hot glue sticks
craft glue
scissors
paintbrush
acrylic paint
paper doll duplicates
Séance Parlor templates

Follow the sisters "behind the veil"!

The Spiritualist movement reached its peak in the 1920s. Following the human losses of WWI, many grieving family members sought to "reach behind the veil" to make contact with their deceased loved ones. Many unscrupulous individuals saw an opportunity for financial gain, selling the false promise of psychic abilities to eager believers.

Harry Houdini's entry into Spiritualism began as a sincere attempt to contact his dead mother. Appalled by the exploitation he witnessed, he made it his mission to expose the trickery of psychic mediums. Together with *Scientific American* magazine, Houdini offered a generous cash prize to anyone who could demonstrate supernatural abilities. The prize remains unclaimed.

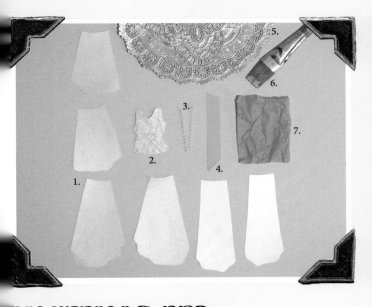

MATERIALS: REO

1. The Paper Studio® Silver Vellum Paper
2. The Paper Studio® Crinkle Cream Paper
3. The Paper Studio® Gemstones Small Pearl
4. yellow paper
5. gold doily
6. Craft Smart® Acrylic Paint Citron
7. orange tissue paper

MATERIALS: LUCILLE

1. Recollections® Boho Die Cut Doilies
2. gold doily
3. blue sequin craft canvas material (Hobby Lobby.
4. The Paper Studio® Silver Vellum Paper
5. white feather
6. royal blue paint
7. The Paper Studio® Gemstones Small Pearl
8. DecoArt Dazzling Metallics®Acrylic Paint Purple Pearl
9. thin black ribbon
10. Celebrate It® Luxe Wired Edge Velvet Ribbon (royal blue)
11. Sei Midnight Velvet Paper

1. Run a thin line of hot glue down Reo's right abdomen. Place the shirt piece so that its edge lines up with the right side of her body.

2. Push the unglued edge of the shirt towards the center of the doll's abdomen and secure it with hot glue. This should cause the bodice piece to buckle out in the middle.

3. Point your hot glue gun up into the bottom of Reo's shirt, applying a bit of glue. Before it cools, push the middle of the shirt into the glue, creating two ridges.

4. Fold the pieces of Reo's skirt into pleats.

5. Attach the shortest pleated skirt piece to Reo's left hip with hot glue, wrapping the fold around her hip.

6. Attach the second pleated skirt piece next to the first, using hot glue. From Reo's left to right, the skirt pieces should be getting longer.

7. Attach the third pleated skirt piece beside the first two, using hot glue.

8. Attach the longest pleated skirt pieces to the *back* of the doll with hot glue, creating the illusion that the skirt lengthens and wraps around. If necessary, you can always cut, pleat, and attach more skirt pieces.

9. Pick sections of your doily that will work nicely for the waist and collar of Reo's dress. Snip out your chosen pieces.

10. Use craft glue to attach the hip piece(s) so that the white side of the doily is facing up. Wrap the ends of the hip piece around the doll and secure with glue.

11. Repeat step 10 for the collar of Reo's dress, wrapping the ends of the collar piece around her shoulders.

12. Using a medium/large soft-bristle paintbrush, cover Reo's dress with a *thin* layer of the citron green paint. Long, quick sweeps of the paintbrush will keep the paint from getting streaky.

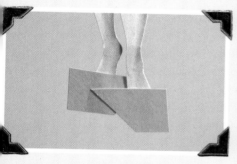

13. Glue snippets of yellow paper to Reo's feet.

14. Trim the yellow paper around the shape of Reo's feet to create shoes.

15. Use craft glue to attach thin snippets of yellow paper to Reo's ankles.

16. Trim the snippets of yellow paper so that they are flush with Reo's ankle. Add heels if desired using another snippet of the yellow paper.

17. Create two pompoms for the shoes by crumpling two .5" x .5" pieces of orange tissue paper.

18. Use craft glue to attach the pompoms and then paint a small green dot in their center.

Séance Parlor: Reo

19. Create a long strand of pearls by attaching two strands of adhesive scrapbooking gems in a long "v" shape down the neckline.

20. Make your doll dance the Charleston by cutting and repositioning her legs!

21. Give your doll a more suitable flapper haircut!

Séance Parlor: Lucille

1. From your colorful doily, cut a piece that will look nice at the neckline of Lucille's dress.

2. Flex the piece of doily so that it has a bit of dimension.

3. Use hot glue to glue the doily into place at the neckline, retaining its dimension.

4. Pleat the two skirt pieces and attach them with hot glue to Lucille's hips, wrapping them slightly around the doll.

5. Glue the dress piece to the doll, over the pleated skirt pieces.

6. Use scissors to create a fringe on the bottom of the dress piece.

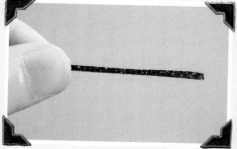

7. When you are finished, the entire bottom of the dress piece should be fringed.

8. Cut strips of the same material you used for your dress, making them as thin as the fringe you created in steps 6-7.

9. Use craft glue to attach these strips to the dress so that they are overlapping the pleated skirt pieces. Six to seven strips should do the trick.

10. From your gold doily, cut a bit of ornament that will look nice at the hip of Lucille's dress.

11. Glue the doily pieces to Lucille's dress so that the white is facing up.

12. Using a medium/large soft-bristle paintbrush, cover any white parts of Lucille's dress with a *thin* layer of purple/blue paint. Long, quick sweeps of the paintbrush will keep the paint from getting streaky.

13. Repeat steps 13-16 of Reo's How-To to create Lucille's shoes from the black velvet paper.

14. Use craft glue to attach a very thin ribbon to Lucille's head. Something with a little sparkle works nicely!

15. Finish Lucille's flapper headband by adding a few strands from a white feather. If you can avoid burning yourself, hot glue may be the best adhesive for this step.

Design Your Own Paper Fashions

MATERIALS:

a good story	cardstock paper	hot glue gun
fashion research	No. 2 pencil	hot glue sticks
family photos	decorative papers	craft glue
photocopier	embellishments	paint
tracing paper	lace	paintbrush
	ribbon	scissors

Maybe your grandma rode bareback on a white horse at the Chicago World's Fair, or maybe she bakes the best oatmeal chocolate chip cookies in the world. Whatever her special talent, recreating her stories in miniature is a lovely tribute!

Once you are comfortable with the techniques explored in the How-Tos, you can adapt them for use in your original designs. There are two different ways to approach this. You can come up with new combinations of the provided pattern pieces, *or* you can create *new* pattern pieces, using paper dolls, family photos, or fashion photographs as templates. I'll be illustrating this technique with the help of my Grandma Pat on her wedding day.

Before You Begin

Since you will need to trace over your photograph, you may want to use a copy rather than the original, especially if the original is old and fragile. If the photograph you have chosen is small, you can use your photocopier's enlargement settings to make it bigger.

When designing a paper dress from a photograph, it helps to have some sense of the original dress's construction—photographs of the garment from different angles will be helpful. Better yet, take a look at the actual dress, or look for images of similar clothing from the era. The way clothing is constructed is particular to its time, so other garments will provide clues. Where is the garment fitted or full? Where does the waist fall? Old sewing patterns can help this process.

1-2. Use a pencil and tracing paper to make a basic outline of the garment.

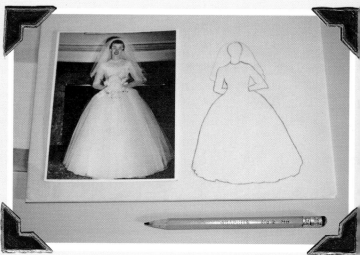

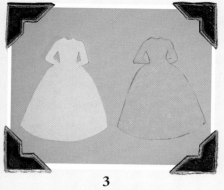

3

4

3. Transfer your outline to cardstock by tracing it and cut it out. This will be the foundation to sculpt your design. You can always sculpt your creation directly onto copies of Lucille and Reo, as you did in the How-Tos, but this method will let you experiment with body shapes and replicate the pose from your chosen photograph.

4. Place a fresh piece of tracing paper over your outline from step 2. Now is the time to put your fashion research to use, adding the dress's technical details. Think of the garment you are copying as a puzzle whose pieces are fabric. You are working backwards from the complete "puzzle" in your photograph, trying to determine how its shapes fit together to make a whole. Wherever you see sewing in the original garment, add a corresponding pencil line to your outline.

Mark things such as where the sleeves are sewn to the bodice and where the bodice attaches to the skirt. If the skirt is full, you can add lines where there are large folds, or keep it a simple bell shape (see the *Family Parlor* and Reo's *New Orleans* How-Tos for their approaches to skirt construction). The placement of any darts in the original garment is a good guide for retaining dimension in your paper version.

5–6. Now with your understanding of the garment's construction, you will create the individual pattern pieces. Go over your technical outline from step 4 using a fresh piece of tracing paper to duplicate each segment, tracing (separately) the sleeves, bodice, skirt, and other details you want to include.

5

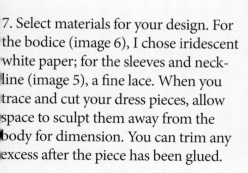

6

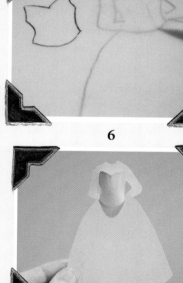

7

7. Select materials for your design. For the bodice (image 6), I chose iridescent white paper; for the sleeves and neckline (image 5), a fine lace. When you trace and cut your dress pieces, allow space to sculpt them away from the body for dimension. You can trim any excess after the piece has been glued.

8. Use techniques mastered in the How-Tos—and your own—to sculpt an original design!

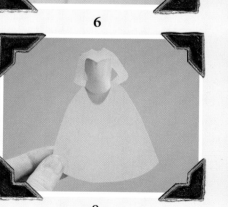

8

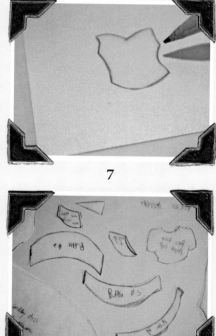

9

9. Designing your paper dress will require trial and error. Whenever I tackle a new garment, it takes several tries to get the pattern pieces and materials just right. But it's always worth the effort!

Accessorize!

The ladies of the past knew a thing or two about dressing with *flair,* and the world of vintage accessories is quirky, colorful, and coquette! With hats, gloves, nylons, costume jewelry, and furs to choose from, the dress is only the beginning. In the following pages, you'll find ideas for embellishing your dolls further. As with your paper draping, look to real vintage accessories for ideas!

Century Girl Vintage, New Orleans 2016

Century Girl Vintage, New Orleans 2016

Handbag

1. Cut a rectangular piece of paper.
2. Hot glue a bit of cotton batting and a looped chain to the back of the paper.
3. Fold the paper over the cotton and glue. Trim the corners and add a thin line of metallic paint to the top.

Frills & Furbelows

A fun way to jazz up a frock or accessory is with tissue paper bows or pompoms. These particular frills require very little material! A tiny square of tissue paper will do. Simply crumple it into a ball, or tie a thread around its center and snip to shape.

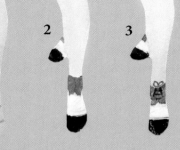

Shoes

1. Draw.
2. Paint.
3. Embellish!

Shoes for your paper doll are as fetching as they are easy to create! My favorite method is to draw the lines of the shoe onto the foot with pencil. After I am satisfied with this "sketch," I paint over it with acrylic paint using a finely tipped paintbrush. After the paint has dried, I add embellishments. There is no limit to the materials you can embellish with: ribbon, adhesive gemstones, tulle, and gold paper, just to name a few!

Corsage

Ruffles

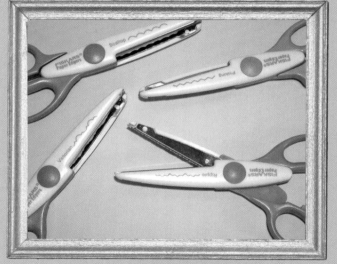

Gloves

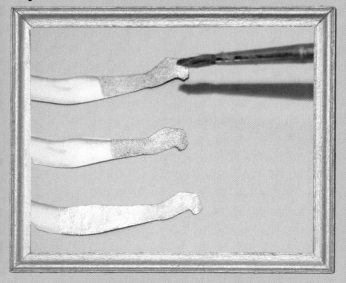

Coiffure

Jewels The old armoire contained costume jewelry. Create your own using everything from broken jewelry to old Christmas ornaments. For more complicated pieces, draw the shape in pencil before tracing it with a metallic gel pen. Use liquid craft glue and a finely tipped paintbrush to attach decorations. Materials are listed, with earring materials *italicized*.

Gold gel pen
Green nail polish

Recollections™ Rhinestone Sheet
The Paper Studio® Chevron Gemstones
Liquid Pearls™ Dimensional Paint

Gold gel pen
Broken Christmas ornament
The Paper Studio® gemstone

Gold gel pen
Key charm from Etsy
(nicoledebruin)

Gold gel pen
Miniaturized photo

The Paper Studio® Adhesive Pearl

Gold doily
The Paper Studio® Gemstones
Liquid Pearls™ Dimensional Paint

Gold gel pen
Heart nail decal

The Paper Studio® Gemstones
The Paper Studio® Sticker Border

Millinery

Throughout the decades, Lucille and Reo wore many hats. With a few silk flower petals and bits of embellishment, you can create a hat collection that any queen would envy! My favorite method of millinery is to choose a flower petal and shape it around the doll's head, trimming and hot gluing. The materials appear below each hat.

White paper flower petal
Snippet of white antique lace

Peach-colored silk flower petal
Snippet of plastic green leaf
Silk daisy petal
Blue silk flower petal

The Paper Studio® Gemstones
Green feather
Liquid Pearls™ Dimensional Paint

Yellow silk flower petal
White tulle
White feather

Red velvet flower petal
Striped ribbon
Blue tissue paper bow

Green silk flower petal
White flower petal
Pink flower petal

Play

Texture

One of the best things that historical fashion has to offer is *texture*. As you look through a rack of clothing at a vintage store, you will encounter silk, satin, feathers, velvet, and fur, to name just a few. Using feathers is one way to achieve a "fur" texture in miniature; felt is another. Feathers also make great boas to accessorize your flapper looks!

Century Girl Vintage, New Orleans 2016

Paper Clip Hangers

1

2

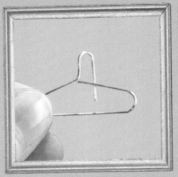

3

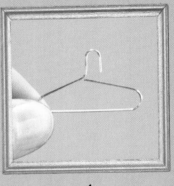

4

One way to display your beautiful paper dresses is on hangers created from paper clips! 1. Begin with a #1-size metal paper clip. 2. Bend the paper clip's prongs outward. 3. Using pliers, create a sharp angle in the paper clip's longer prong. 4. Trim the ends of the paper clip as shown. Use craft glue or hot glue to secure your garments to the paper clip.

Miniature Stage

A stage is easy to create using two hardcover books, a clothespin, and free backdrops downloaded from **www.LadyDelaney.com**! Print the backdrop onto cardstock paper and secure it to the open books as shown in the picture on the left.

The Old Armoire:

Easy to make & perfect for storing your pretty paper creations!

Create your own using:

- cardstock photocopy of armoire
- **X-ACTO®** blade
- scissors
- paintbrush
- acrylic paint (brown + black)
- cardboard tea box
- cardboard scraps
- craft glue

1. Make a color photocopy of this page using cardstock or heavyweight paper.

2. Cut out the armoire copy and use an **X-ACTO®** blade to make three cuts along the doors, as shown.

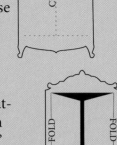

3. Fold the doors outward, creasing them along their "hinges."

4. Use the **X-ACTO®** blade and scissors to cut a rectangular piece out of the larger side of the tea box—about 4"x 5", or approximately the same size as the opening in your armoire copy when its doors are open.

5. Use craft glue to attach your armoire cutout to the tea box, lining up their openings.

6. Cut two back "legs" from your cardboard scraps. Attach them to the back of the tea box with craft glue. Set the armoire on its back while the glue dries.

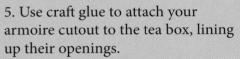

7. After the glue has dried, trim the back legs so they are even with the front legs and the armoire can stand upright.

8. Cover the cardboard legs and any visible tea box areas with paint.

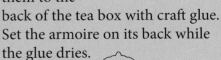

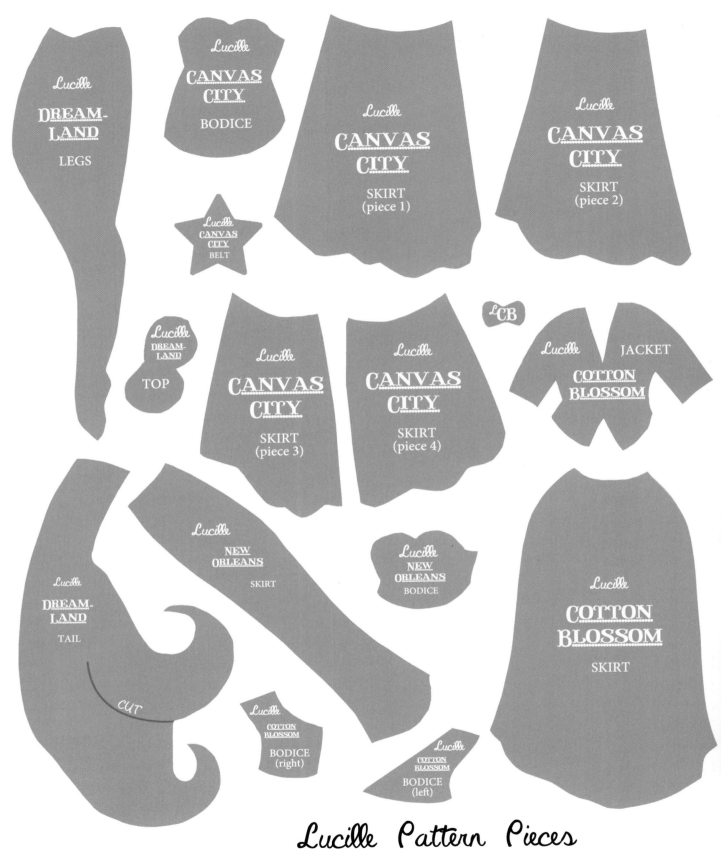

Lucille Pattern Pieces

Don't Forget!

—Photocopy or trace these pattern pieces *and* the paper dolls *before* beginning the How-Tos.

—"Right" and "left" are used in relation to the doll's body, not the crafter's.

—When tracing, the text side of your pattern should always face the *back* of your paper.

—Pattern pieces are sized slightly larger than the dolls.

—For more information on getting started, flip to the *Before You Begin* section.

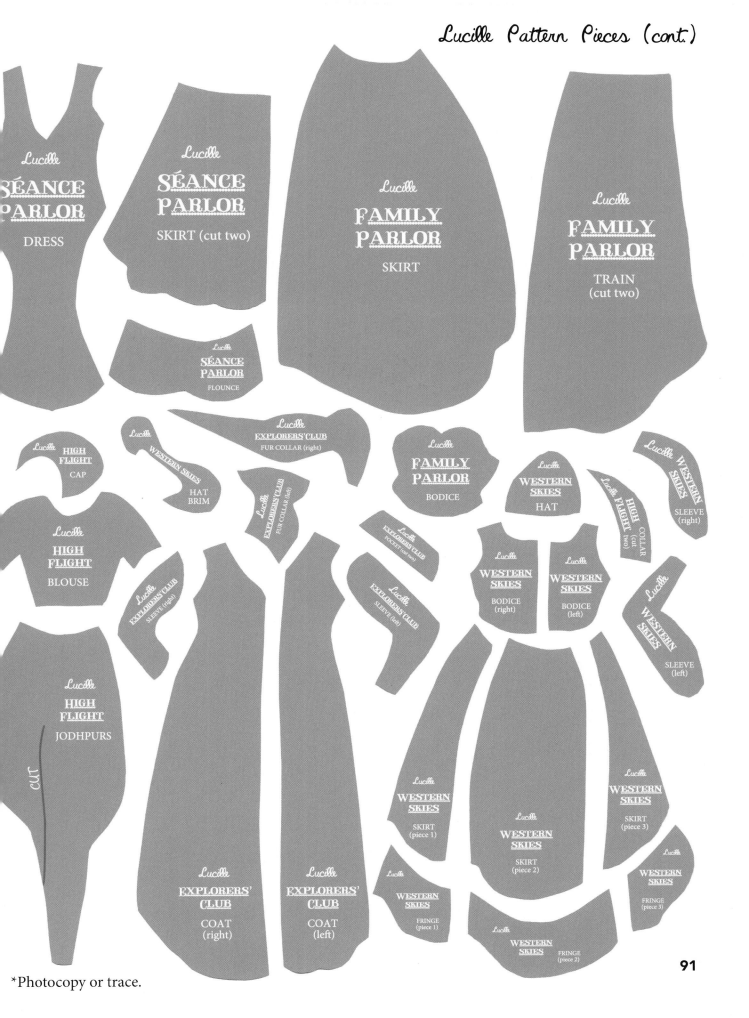

Lucille
SÉANCE PARLOR
DRESS

Lucille
SÉANCE PARLOR
SKIRT (cut two)

Lucille
SÉANCE PARLOR
FLOUNCE

Lucille
FAMILY PARLOR
SKIRT

Lucille
FAMILY PARLOR
TRAIN (cut two)

Lucille
HIGH FLIGHT
CAP

Lucille
WESTERN SKIES
HAT BRIM

Lucille
EXPLORERS' CLUB
FUR COLLAR (right)

Lucille
EXPLORERS' CLUB
FUR COLLAR (left)

Lucille
EXPLORERS' CLUB
POCKET (cut two)

Lucille
FAMILY PARLOR
BODICE

Lucille
WESTERN SKIES
HAT

Lucille
HIGH FLIGHT
COLLAR (cut two)

Lucille
WESTERN SKIES
SLEEVE (right)

Lucille
HIGH FLIGHT
BLOUSE

Lucille
EXPLORERS' CLUB
SLEEVE (right)

Lucille
EXPLORERS' CLUB
SLEEVE (left)

Lucille
WESTERN SKIES
BODICE (right)

Lucille
WESTERN SKIES
BODICE (left)

Lucille
WESTERN SKIES
SLEEVE (left)

Lucille
HIGH FLIGHT
JODHPURS

cut

Lucille
EXPLORERS' CLUB
COAT (right)

Lucille
EXPLORERS' CLUB
COAT (left)

Lucille
WESTERN SKIES
SKIRT (piece 1)

Lucille
WESTERN SKIES
SKIRT (piece 2)

Lucille
WESTERN SKIES
SKIRT (piece 3)

Lucille
WESTERN SKIES
FRINGE (piece 1)

Lucille
WESTERN SKIES
FRINGE (piece 2)

Lucille
WESTERN SKIES
FRINGE (piece 3)

*Photocopy or trace.

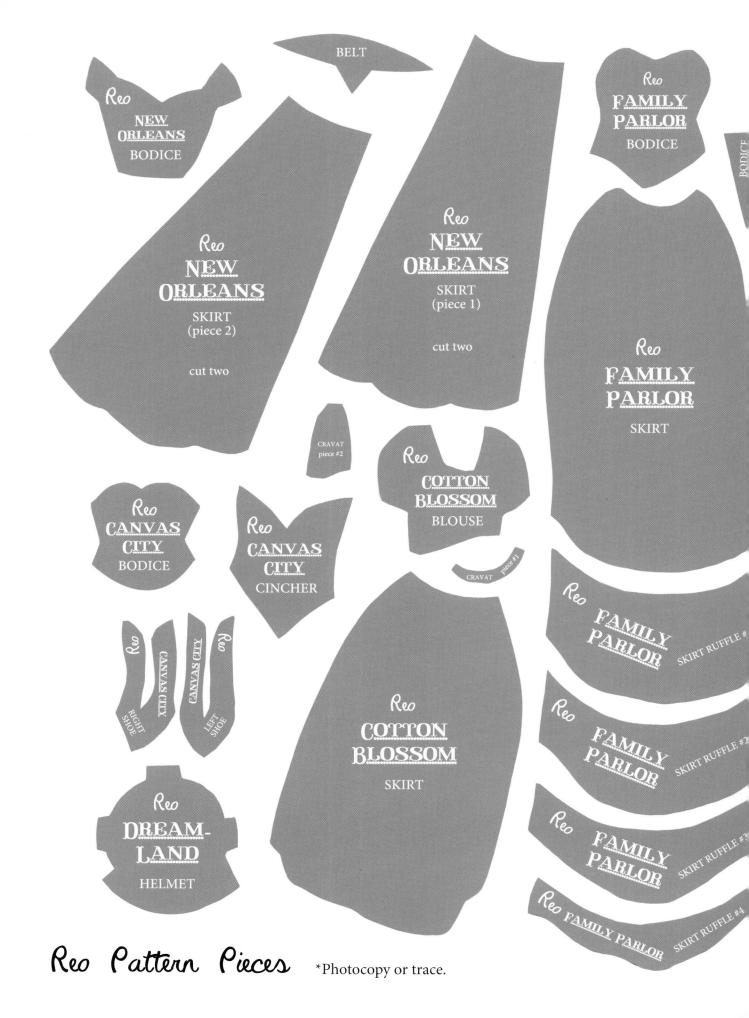

BELT

Reo **NEW ORLEANS** BODICE

Reo **NEW ORLEANS** SKIRT (piece 2) cut two

Reo **NEW ORLEANS** SKIRT (piece 1) cut two

Reo **FAMILY PARLOR** BODICE

BODICE

Reo **FAMILY PARLOR** SKIRT

CRAVAT piece #2

Reo **COTTON BLOSSOM** BLOUSE

CRAVAT piece #1

Reo **CANVAS CITY** BODICE

Reo **CANVAS CITY** CINCHER

Reo **FAMILY PARLOR** SKIRT RUFFLE #

Reo CANVAS CITY RIGHT SHOE

CANVAS CITY *Reo* LEFT SHOE

Reo **COTTON BLOSSOM** SKIRT

Reo **FAMILY PARLOR** SKIRT RUFFLE #2

Reo **DREAM-LAND** HELMET

Reo **FAMILY PARLOR** SKIRT RUFFLE #3

Reo **FAMILY PARLOR** SKIRT RUFFLE #4

Reo Pattern Pieces *Photocopy or trace.

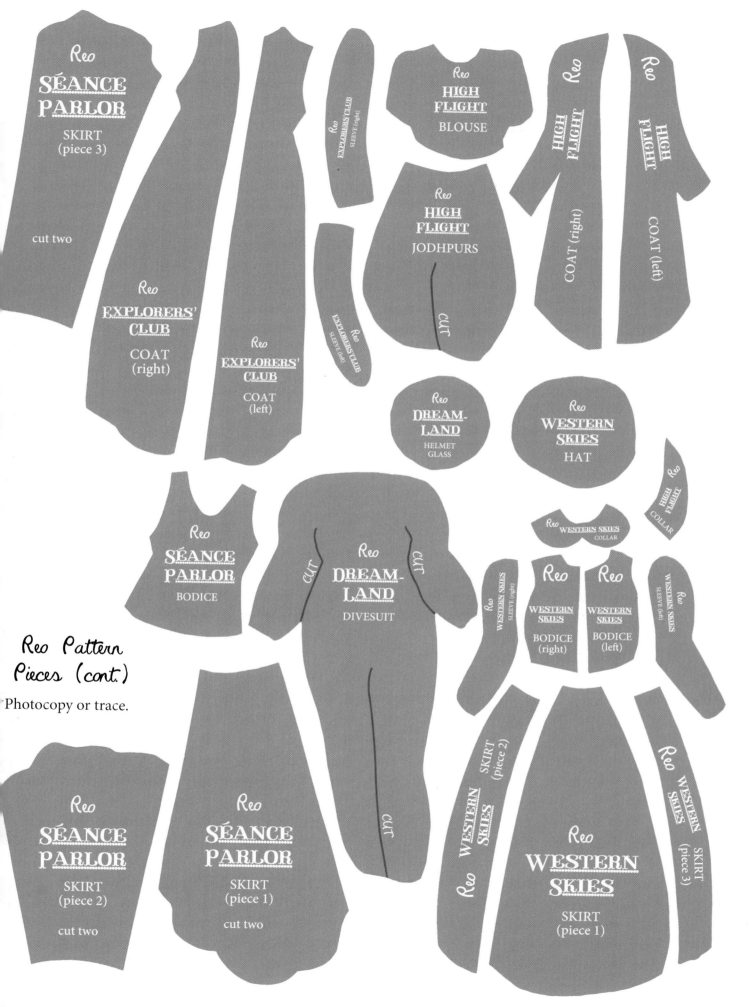

Reo Pattern
Pieces (cont.)

Photocopy or trace.

Resources for the paper fashionista...

Get Exploring!

Stateside:
Black Fashion Museum (DC)
A Century of Hats (Savannah)
The Charleston Museum
The Costume Institute (NYC)
Cowgirl Museum and Hall of Fame
(Fort Worth)
FIT Museum (NYC)
LACMA (Los Angeles)
Louisiana State Museum
Philadelphia Museum of Art
Ringling Circus Museum (FL)
RISD Museum (Providence)
SCAD Fash (Savannah)
Smithsonian (DC)
Women of the West Museum
(Denver)

Europe & Beyond
Fashion & Textile Museum
(London)
Musée et Jardin Christian
Dior
(Granville)
Musée Galliera (Paris)
V&A Museum (London)
Mode Museum (Antwerp)
Bath Fashion Museum
Balenciaga Museum (Getaria)
Gucci Museum (Florence)
Palazzo Fortuny (Venice)
Bata Shoe Museum (Toronto)
Kyoto Fashion Institute
Museo Frida Kahlo (Mexico City)

Get Inspired!

Digital Fashion History
www.bergfashionlibrary.com
www.costume.org
www.digitalcollections.nypl.org
www.nwhm.org
www.pinterest.com
www.tyrannyofstyle.com
www.vam.ac.uk
www.vintagefashionguild.org
www.vintagetextile.com

Required Reading (by author):
Francois Boucher
Alison Gernsheim
Edith Head
Anne Hollander
Robert Hudovernik
Lucy Johnston
Melissa Leventon
the Seeberger Brothers
Valerie Steele
Caroline Weber
Joshua Zeitz

(by publisher):
Kyoto Costume Institute
Metropolitan Museum of Art
Sears Roebuck
Smithsonian
Taschen
Victoria and Albert

Get to Work!

Crafting Materials:
AC Moore
Dick Blick
Goodwill/Salvation Army
Hobby Lobby
JoAnn Fabric and Craft
Marshalls/TJ Maxx
Michaels
Papyrus

Crafting Materials (Online Retailers):
www.AcornSpring.com
www.Amazon.com
www.CastleintheAir.biz
www.CreateforLess.com
www.Etsy.com
www.FactoryDirectCraft.com
www.Fiskars.com
www.MisterArt.com
MulberryPaperandMore.com
www.NYCentralArt.com
www.OrientalTrading.com
www.PaperMart.com
www.PaperSource.com
www.ShopAngelaLiguori.com
www.Vintage-Ornaments.com

Miniature Decor:
www.Ebay.com
www.LadyDelaney.com
www.Miniatures.com

Don't forget to seek out local resources. Every town has its own shops specializing in antiques, art supplies, and artisanal papers.

Special thanks to a few of my favorite local businesses who helped with materials and inspiration:

CENTURY GIRL VINTAGE
New Orleans, LA

THE GET-UP VINTAGE
Ann Arbor, MI

KALAMAZOO ANTIQUE MALL
Kalamazoo, MI

KALAMAZOO BOOK ARTS CENTER
Kalamazoo, MI

LILI VINTAGE BOUTIQUE
New Orleans, LA

ONCE UPON A TIME ANTIQUES
Boise, ID

PAPER AND PETAL
Kalamazoo, MI

PROMENADE FINE FABRICS
New Orleans, LA

About the Author

Lauren is the creator of the Etsy sensation **L. Delaney Miniatures.** Born and raised in Kalamazoo, Michigan, she works and plays in Michigan, New York—and a haunted mansion in New Orleans' Garden District. She often wanders off the beaten path, frolicking in vintage and chasing ghosts. Lauren also designs for stage and film and has displayed her work in Tiffany & Co. windows as well as the National Building Museum.

www.LadyDelaney.com   **f** @theladydelaney   📷 @lady delaney

She wishes to thank...

Mom, whose beautiful Halloween costumes were better than all the sparkle of Broadway. She watched as we loved them to pieces in the backyard, and has cheered loudly for us ever since.

Dad, fashion pioneer of yellow suits and knee-high black socks—and a generous and loving parent.

Murt G., for his brain, which is a delight.

Maria, for providing the Broadway soundtrack to our lives.

Grandpa Geno and Grandma Kate, who started it all.

Grandpa Bill and Grandma Pat, for my dad, and all the wonderful aunts and uncles.

Bobby Danner and the staff of the Olivier House Hotel, for their generous hospitality upon my arrival in New Orleans, and their friendship ever since.

Jill and Beth Burzin, the truest squirrelfriends a gal could ask for.

Matthew Morris and Andrew Farrier, two of the world's finest storytellers, for a friendship which opens my eyes to new wonders. And Matthew, again, for his help with edits.

John Preble, lunatic proprietor of the Abita Springs Mystery House, mentor & friend.

My Etsy customers, whose generous support changed the course of my life.

Nate, for feeding, loving, and inspiring me.

The countless others enriching my life & appearing in these pages in their various disguises.

My parents, again, for believing in me and encouraging my weirdness.